What clients a
Rico Peña's sell

"Regardless of how you started, or where you are now in your career, Rico Peña will empower you to take the next step. A master of communication and marketing, Rico has assembled an incredible team to help you package yourself with an irresistible image. Rico has unique insight to see the final product and create the step-by-step process to put your business on top. Check out The Client Nation. *It's your first step towards ultimate success."*

DAWN PICI, COO AND CO-FOUNDER PICI & PICI INC.
COAUTHOR OF THE BESTSELLING BOOKS
SELL NAKED ON THE PHONE AND
SELL NAKED IN PERSON
(WWW.PICIANDPICI.COM)

"Rico, just wanted to say a huge thank you for Joy of Connecting day. I LOVED it and learned so much from you. You have a way with words. I hope to be at many more of your meetings in the future. Thank you again for a fantastic day."

ANNE LANEY, CEO AND FOUNDER
SASSY SATCHELS

"Rico, I came to your workshop as a new person to network marketing. I was very nervous and unsure of myself. I am just starting out in the company and, although I believe in the products, I was clueless. You were amazing. I came away from your workshop with a confidence I never had before, a plan for networking, and joy in my heart from meeting new people and friends. You showed me how to step out of the box. You set goals before me and you showed me how to have FUN in the midst of it. I thank you very much for the knowledge you presented, the gifts you offered each of us, and the opportunity to learn more."

LINDA LJAMASTER
ZOÉ LIFE

"Rico is an innovative, knowledgeable, and personable business marvel with strong marketing insights. His creativity, drive and foresight to continually develop successful start-up businesses are inspiring. Rico's business success is a great model for what Zig Ziglar says: "If you can dream it, then you can achieve it. You will get all you want in life if you help enough other people get what they want." Rico continues to thrive personally and professionally because he knows how to help others achieve greatness."

MICHELLE STIDWELL
PROFESSIONAL TRAINER, COACH, CONSULTANT, AND INDEPENDENT CONTRACTOR
KNOWLEDGE WORKS GROUP

"Rico has been one of the most inspiring individuals I have ever worked with in my career history. I personally have been on the receiving end of his consultation expertise for my business ventures. He has an outstanding work ethic, a discerning eye and ear for success concerning his client base, and a list of triumphs in business that few could compare to. I would recommend him for personal coaching for small businesses all the way to the top of the Fortune 500 list."

REANN RING, CEO AND FOUNDER
SAFIRE PRODUCTIONS & GLAMOUR TAGS

"Rico has an amazing vision to help others in the business world achieve success. With his leadership tools and training events, you can't miss. If you are in the Atlanta area and need coaching, seek out Rico to improve how you run your business."

JOHN LEHMBERG, OWNER
MAKE IT LOUD, INC.

"When you need someone you can count on to get results, Rico is the go-to person I always look to first. His new venture—The Speakers Vault—is the homerun of business. Expect Rico to be your friend and your growth link! He is mine . . ."

GEORGE ISHEE, CEO,
SMALL STEPS TO BIG RESULTS

"Rico is one of those special individuals that you definitely want to work with. He deeply listens to and focuses on your needs. I have rarely worked with such an outstanding person and would give him my highest recommendation to anyone seeking the services that Rico provides. Top qualities: Great Results, Personable, High Integrity."

STEPHEN ROSNER, CEO AND FOUNDER
THE GOAL GETTERS

"Rico is a great leader and entrepreneur with incredible customer service skills and a joy to work with on any business venture. Top qualities: Expert, High Integrity, Creative."

RICK DUDA, REAL ESTATE AGENT AND CEO AND FOUNDER
HOMES DESIGNED TO SELL

"Rico is very knowledgeable in marketing and sales. He aggressively works to achieve his goals and strategically encourages his clients towards theirs. He is upbeat, energetic, and personable. Rico has been a pleasure to work with."

SHIRLEY VOORHEES, CEO AND FOUNDER
TITUS2

"Rico is the most talented marketing professional I've dealt with in 16 years of being a professional trainer and speaker. He has an incredible ability to package and market your business with outstanding results. His creative genius allows him to see the possibilities in assisting his clients in increasing their exposure and incomes. He comes with my highest endorsement."

GIOVE PICI, CEO AND CO-FOUNDER, PICI & PICI INC.
COAUTHOR OF THE BESTSELLING BOOK
SELL NAKED ON THE PHONE AND
SELL NAKED IN PERSON
(WWW.PICIANDPICI.COM)

"It is one of the commonest of mistakes to consider that the limit of our power of perception is also the limit of all there is to perceive."

CW. LEADBEATER

The Client Nation

Their PERCEPTION, *Your* PROFITS

What the clients are saying you should do
so they will become loyal repeat clients who refer you

Based on countless client interviews, research and their buying experiences.

The Client Nation

Their PERCEPTION, *Your* PROFITS

Book & Cover design: Debbie Manning
ISBN 978-0-615-38434-4
Publishing support provided by:
Booklogix Publishing Services, Inc.
Alpharetta, Georgia
Printed in United States

To my beautiful bride

Andi

for her unyielding support, amazing patience, and unconditional love.

This book would never have existed if it were not for her belief in me and her loving insistence that I should write it.

Thank you, my love.

"Regardless of where you start, or where you are now in your career,
Rico Pena will empower you to take the next step.
A master of communication and marketing,
Rico has assembled an incredible team
at the Speakers Vault to help you package yourself
with an irresistible image.
Rico has unique insight to see the final product
and create the step by step process to put your business on top.
Check out the Speakers Vault and TSVLive.
It's your first step towards ultimate success."

DAWN PICI,
OWNER, PICI & PICI INC

ACKNOWLEDGEMENTS

I feel honored and humbled to be surrounded by those who have supported me when sometimes I could not see the big picture.

Thank you to my wife ***Andi***, and my incredible children, ***Alex*** and ***Rebecca***, whose support has always be unwavering, no matter what was thrown at us.

Thank you to my wonderful in-laws, ***Jules and Sunny Organ***, for your support and reassuring words.

Thank you to my mentors, ***Joe and Dawn Pici***, who have always inspired me to see beyond my own perception, whose Sell Naked® 3-day boot camps forged the business mind I have today, and who helped me to clearly see my talents and how to use them, which ultimately led to the writing of this book. The *"Living the Dream Tour 2009"* was definitely the crown jewel.

A special thank you to my editors ***Cindy Elsberry*** whose amazing wordsmith abilities overcame miles of run-on sentences. She reshaped deep thoughts, making them simple, understandable, and valuable to all who read them. To my copyright editor ***Nanette Littlestone,*** whose relentless drive for perfection details and quality resulted in a product that was beyond my expectation. Thank you for believing in my message and for your talents that made my message come to life.

A special thanks to ***Abbey Hout of Pink Ink Media*** and ***Debbie Sheppard*** from the ***Tony Jeary High Performance Resource*** team for all the graphic design, book cover, and layout. Thank you for an amazing job.

"Vision is the
art of seeing what is invisible to others."

JONATHAN SWIFT

PREFACE

When you picked up this book, you may have wondered, *"What is this book about?"* but what you really thought was, *"Is this book worth my time and money?"*

Good question!

In any business, big or small, starting or established, there is one common denominator that can make the difference between success and an "out of business" sign: ***the client.*** Without clients there are no sales; no sales, no cash flow; no cash flow, no business.

As a specialist in human behavior and an with 25 years experience in relational sales, I have taught and consulted corporations and individuals. I have offered them a type of leverage other professions cannot—the client's perception and how to connect to it.

Let me ask you . . .

- Would your business benefit if you could know what your client was thinking?
- How often do you find yourself explaining what you do versus profiting from it?
- What would you pay to have your clients fall in love with your product or service and tell everyone about it?

By reading and applying the information in this book you will be able to:

1. Make your product or service enticing to every client.
2. Create a referral machine that will drive more new business.
3. Increase your closing ratios and loyal repeat client base.

More importantly, the above results are not based on theory or outdated information. They are the culmination of countless interviews, focus groups, and research in an exhaustive search for the truth on what clients really want and seek from businesses when they buy and refer. They will tell you their perceptions and experiences, why they buy, how they decide, and why they refer.

This book was created to provide the business owner, salesperson, or individual direct sales professional unique insight into the client's perception in his own words, thoughts, and experiences. ***The Client Nation*** was created by the client as an inside look into what you, as a business owner, need to know to earn his trust, loyalty, repeat business and, most importantly, the client's voice.

I wrote this book after 20 years of working with many individuals, businesses, and focus groups, and seeing the same challenges time and again. (Not to mention my wife's constant, loving insistence to do so. I am so glad she did.) The main question for most of the individuals, business owners, and direct market companies that I trained was, "How do I clearly communicate the value of my business so my clients are inspired to buy and promote me?" That question led to a search for the answer from the one group that could answer it clearly and honestly: *the clients.* This is the one true common denominator that can make or break any company, no matter how big or small it is. If a business does not have clients, it has no profits or cash flow and therefore no business.

Isn't it important to understand the needs, benefits, or solutions for the one single element that determines the success or failure of your business? Then provide them? You would think so. Yet this happens less than one would imagine and not just by individuals and small or medium companies. You will see it is the lack of understanding of the client's perceived value that makes what seems a simple equation of supply and demand a complicated solution. It amazes me to see how certain businesses today assume they know what the client needs better than the client does. This company then wonders why it went out of business or lost a large market share.

As you will learn and experience in ***The Client Nation***, once you know how to create the client's specific comfort zones and provide the right solutions for that perception, you will begin to accomplish the results you seek in your business. By not understanding our own needs, fears, and priorities, we tend to operate from a *survival mode,* which will most likely cost sales. You will also learn how to identify what makes each client "tick," then better serve that client and create more sales and referrals with little to no effort.

To me, there is no greater joy than to see the passion and enthusiasm—once lost by frustration, fear, and disappointment—shine in those who find clarity and understanding. I hope this book does the same for you. I wish you great prosperity and success in all your endeavors.

RICO PEÑA

"Ideas are the beginning points of all fortunes"

NAPOLEON HILL

Table of Contents

Foreword ix

Introduction xi

CHAPTER 1: The Art of Communication 1

- Is Social Media a Fad?
- The Power of the Digital Voice
- The Power of Words
- You Speaka the Client?
- The Most Difficult Question

CHAPTER 2: The Language of Client 9

- Perceived Value
- Features vs. Benefits
- Your Target Audience
- Mindset
- You Wear What You Think
- The Proverbial Fork in the Road
- Survival Mode
- Servant Mindset
- Take Your Mindset Temperature
- In Business for the Client

CHAPTER 3: The Clarity of Perception 41

- Walk a Mile in My Shoes
- Emotion to Logic
- Relational Business
- Understanding Human Behavior

CHAPTER 4: The Four Regions of *the Client Nation* 55

- The Comfort Zone
- Natural Tendencies
- An Inside Look
- The Client's Pace
- The Client's Priorities
- The Four Quadrants

CHAPTER 5: The **DOMINANT** Region 71

- Speaking the **DOMINANT** Client's Language
- Words that Describe a **D**
- Blind Spots
- Selling to a High **D**
- Coaching Points
- What **DOMINANT** Clients Are Saying

CHAPTER 6: The **INTERACTIVE** Region 83

- Identifying the **INTERACTIVE** Client
- Words that Describe an **I**

- Speaking the **INTERACTIVE** Client's Language
- Selling to an **I** Client
- Blind Spots
- Coaching Points
- What **INTERACTIVE** Clients Are Saying

CHAPTER 7: The STEADY Region 93

- Speaking the **STEADY** Client's Language
- Words that Describe an **S**
- Selling to a **STEADY** Client
- Blind Spots
- Coaching Points
- What **STEADY** Clients Are Saying

CHAPTER 8: The CALCULATING Region 105

- Speaking the **CALCULATING** Client's Language
- Words that Describe a **C**
- Selling to a **CALCULATING** Client
- Blind Spots
- Coaching Points
- What **CALCULATING** Clients Are Saying

CHAPTER 9: Reading Your Client 117

- Body Language
- Vocal Tones

Appendix A 127

Appendix B 129

Appendix C 133

Glossary 137

About the Author 139

FOREWORD

This is the book you have been waiting for! In ***The Client Nation*** Rico and Andi Peña will show you how to increase your bottom line by building long-lasting, profitable relationships with your clients, (even those clients who seem most difficult). We're Joe and Dawn Pici and we have been in the speaking and training industry since 1993. Over that time we have met, listened to, and instructed thousands of speakers, trainers and authors, yet none have impressed us more than Rico and Andi.

We first met the Peñas in July of 2006 when we were keynote speakers at an event they were attending in Atlanta, Georgia. During conversation over dinner one evening, we realized that we shared similar philosophies and recognized Rico as an expert in the area of human behavior and how it relates to marketing. We were very fortunate to be able to experience Rico's training over the next two years as we shared platforms at various events. We always came away from his sessions with an increased focus on the client's perception.

We realized Rico had the ability to help business owners secure loyal, repeat business while cultivating new markets. We were so impressed by his powerful message and engaging delivery style that we contracted him to do multiple engagements for our sales training company, Pici & Pici Inc. Rico always received rave reviews and outstanding evaluations from participants and is equally effective training in both English and Spanish.

It is an honor and privilege to write the forward to a book that will truly improve the effectiveness of everyone who reads it. This book represents Rico's fundamental philosophy of understanding what your clients *really* want. The information in ***The Client Nation*** has helped others skyrocket their businesses and improve their bottom lines through understanding and recognizing what makes their clients tick. Rico will show you how to build lasting relationships that produce more sales, greater loyalty, and quality referrals. This is information that produces RESULTS!

JOE AND DAWN PICI
Pici & Pici Inc.
Accomplish More Through Rapport Mastery[s]

INTRODUCTION

You are about to enter a land of opportunity, wealth, and prosperity. This land is ***the Client Nation.***

This book will provide you with the map to tap into the power of the client's perceptions. You will receive access to the virtual gold mine that represents the client's true needs, desires, and emotional triggers, guided by the client himself. This book will also arm you with the tools to connect, communicate, and successfully build the rapport that creates loyal repeat customers, ongoing leads and, most of all, a higher perceived value for your product or service. *In short, less work, more clients, greater profits.*

The language of ***the Client Nation*** may not be familiar to you or you may not have had the opportunity to practice it in a while. This book will provide you with the common language and native tongue of the residents in the various regions. You will have the opportunity to learn the language as if you were immersed in their everyday lives, learning from the source directly. This vital information will allow you to act more effectively so every client feels more comfortable to buy your product or service.

The Client Nation will also give you turn-by-turn directions through the highway of what we call "the World of MouthOnomics"—a simple yet understated phenomenon that can increase sales or close business doors.

By harnessing the power of ***the Client Nation*** you arm yourself with vital insights that will separate you from the competition, increase your closing ratio, and create more time to do what you love.

Are you ready to begin?

"Life is like a combination lock;
your goal is to find the right numbers, in the right order,
so you can have anything you want."

BRIAN TRACY

CHAPTER 1

The Art of Communication

"Words are the keys to the heart."

CHINESE PROVERB

Welcome to *the Client Nation*

Population:	6,809,972,000 and growing
Native tongue:	Perceived Value based on Benefits, Results, and Solutions
Governed by:	Behaviors, Pace, and Priority

The people of ***the Client Nation*** decide how, why, and what is sold. Their opinions both influence others and determine the course of products and services. Their voices are heard around the world with just a click of the mouse and the fast movements of their thumbs. They can decide the success or immediate failure of any business idea. Those who ignore the power of ***the Client Nation*** will be reduced to mediocrity and may find it difficult to grow and succeed among its communities.

The Client Nation is not driven by brands or gimmicky commercials. Its people are inspired by individuality, practicality, and the anthem, "WHAT IS IN IT FOR ME?" They make decisions about their products and services by personal recommendations, third-party testimonials, and ratings. Blogs are the voice of the nation, social media its platform, and videos its soapbox, that change the *word*-of-mouth marketing process to the *world-of-mouth* viral marketing phenomenon.

The people of ***the Client Nation*** require a personal touch and face-to-face service that provides a unique and tailored experience that goes beyond their expectations. This book is your passport to the fastest growing market in the world, ***the Client Nation.***

Before entering ***the Client Nation,*** there is one aspect that is imperative to understand: the client's words and how they are shared. These words can, as Tony Jeary says, "Accelerate your business at the speed of life," or they can bring about disaster faster than any natural phenomenon.

Is Social Media a Fad?

From technology to news and music to how we eat, today's life is very fast. We have learned to multi task in order to keep up the pace. Life's informational superhighway can be held in a device in the palm of your hand. Decisions and the sharing of experiences from those decisions take place in seconds. This is why instead of *word-of-mouth* marketing, which used to be typical, today's technology has created the *World of Mouth,* which can affect the economics of your day-to-day business in a positive or a negative way.

Social media brings about a fundamental shift in the way we communicate. It affects our economy and ultimately our business, simply by the sharing of an experience.[1]

- 1 out of 8 couples married in the US last year met via social media
- Facebook added 100 million users in less than 9 months. If it was a country it would be considered the 4th largest country in the world.
- 80% of Twitter usage is on mobile devices that people update anywhere and anytime. Imagine what that means for bad customer experiences.
- There are 200,000,000 blogs. 25% of the search results

---

1 Info provided by Social Economics. View the video at www.Sensationalyou.net/inthe-news

for the world's top 20 brands are links to user-generated content. 34% of bloggers post opinions about products or services. Do you know what they are saying about your product or service?

- 78% of consumers trust peer recommendations. Only 14% trust advertisements.

Referrals are the fastest, most inexpensive way to promote your business. The Nielsen rating and marketing system conducted a study and found that over 80% of all buying decisions were made by recommendations, testimonials or ratings.

To understand how the World of Mouth phenomenon can really help your business skyrocket or create the kind of publicity that will make the arrow on your P&L sheet point steeply downwards, let's look into the World of MouthOnomics.

The Power of the Digital Voice

What is the World of MouthOnomics? Sharing experiences about a business, product, or service. What clients share about their experiences on today's social platforms, as well as to their family and friends, could dictate the financial future of your business, all with the simple click of a button.

AT&T® has a great example of clients using the World of MouthOnomics to communicate without saying a word. In one particular commercial a little girl has lost her dog and posts a "HAVE YOU SEEN MY DOG" flyer with the dog's picture. A young guy sees her sadly walking away with a handful of flyers. He takes a picture of the flyer with his mobile phone and sends it via text to his social group. In minutes the message makes the rounds from friend to friend in the social networks—all ages, types, genders, and locations.

Finally, a teenage girl realizes the dog she is petting is the dog that her friend is texting her about and replies to the person who had sent the original photo. As the heartbroken pet owner returns home from posting her flyers, she looks up and sees a young man on her front porch with her dog. She runs to the dog, calls its name, and the two reunite. This advertisement shows the speed and effectiveness of the World of MouthOnomics in its non-verbal sense. All this was accomplished quickly with social media, the client's digital voice. Imagine what this voice could do for your business. It is not just spoken to friends, families, and neighbors in the traditional sense, but also heard digitally by millions around the world at the "speed of life" with a simple click of a button. This creates a fast lane in the World of MouthOnomics.

The Power of Words

Words can connect and build strong relationships or express disappointment about a product or service to the entire world. With just a mouse click opinions are expressed and shared, decisions made, and business fortunes made or lost. This is the economy of the World of MouthOnomics. As you previously read, social media can have a powerful impact on the economics of your business, however, every entry in any blog, Facebook, Twitter, or email begins with a face-to-face experience with the salesperson, product, or service. What happens in that experience will determine what is said on the social media superhighway.

It is said that the pen is mightier than the sword. For the survival of any business today, there is no greater truth. Do you know what your clients are saying in ***the Client Nation?***

"Words can connect and build strong relationships or express

disappointment about a product or service to the entire world."

Words can be powerful allies if applied correctly and in the right perception. As you journey through ***the Client Nation,*** you will have the tools and information to know when, where, how, and even why to speak the language of client fluently. (The language of client; a language a client understands to help them to know, like, and trust you.)

If you had a way to connect with any client and create a more loyal customer, ongoing referrals, and a higher perceived value for your products or service, would that benefit your business's bottom line?

"What you say to the client
can just as easily inspire what they share with others,
more so than your product or service."

RICO PEÑA

You Speaka the Client?

In ***the Client Nation*** there is one simple and common language everyone understands and uses. Just as you take the time to learn common phrases and words when visiting a foreign country in order to communicate more effectively, this chapter will prepare you to understand and begin to speak the language of Client. First, what is the language of Client?

The language of Client is

> ***CLEAR, SIMPLE*** *statements of the tangible* ***RESULTS*** *a client gets from using your products or services. They are focused on* ***OUTCOMES*** *and stress the business* ***VALUE*** *of your offering.*

Sounds simple, right? As you read on, you will see that our interviews and research revealed it is not as simple as it looks. In fact, we began to notice that what businesses view as benefits, the client sees as merely features that do not inspire sales or even the understanding of what it is the business does. The main reason for this was that most businesses did not understand the client's perception as it pertained to their product or service.

If you could know what the client in front of you was thinking, would that help your sales? What you are about to read is exactly, without question, what clients have told us they were thinking at the time they were being sold to or preparing to purchase.

"They are not interested in what you do;

they are interested in what problem

you can solve for them or their company."

"What is in it for me?" That is all the client is interested in. If you cannot ***clearly*** demonstrate value in the client's perception, the likelihood of a sale or referral goes way down. So how do you give the client what he wants? Simply by knowing how to answer the most difficult question we all face in business.

The Most Difficult Question

It seems that as the economy becomes more uncertain, so does the ability to clearly define what we do. So much so, that we spend most of our time explaining what we do versus selling our product or service. Because clients are tightening their grip on disposable income and becoming more specific about where they will spend it, most businesses are struggling to connect with the clients' true needs. Businesses today are trying to decipher where exactly they fit in that short list of specifics in order to get their share of the American dream. Have you ever been to an event where businesses gather to promote their products or services? The intent is to meet new people and tell them what you do and what your business is, while hoping this will interest them enough to buy or use your service, or at the very least provide you with an appointment or a referral. At these events and every day you are in business, you will spend time answering the most difficult question ever asked: "So what do you do?"

It sounds easy to answer this question but it tends to be a very stressful and intimidating experience for some, as the answer can mean a potential payday or lost opportunity. Most networking attendees deal with the fear of the unknown, the stress of rejection, and the lack of confidence about how their products and services will be received. In most cases, they are not sure who their specific client is and what their needs or wants are. The unknown is the reaction of the total stranger to your offering—you do not know her or her business. And the stranger does not know you.

Have you ever watched golf on TV? (Yes, some of you are saying it's painful, but bear with me.) The golfers on TV are the very best in the game. This is what they do for a living—practice and play golf. Yet every time they line up to putt, no matter how often they walk around and look, they are not certain the ball will go in. This is why they are ecstatic when it does go in and upset when it doesn't. You and your business are no different. You know your product or service; you probably know your competition better than your ideal client. What you don't know is who or how to clearly communicate the value to interest the client to buy. Therefore, the client's reaction and if it will generate what you need, is unknown. Just like the golfer, you are leaving your results to chance.

CASE STUDY

I once put just the words "Women's Expo" on my name tag at a networking event. Nothing else. I wanted to see what the reaction would be. I had more people stop me and ask me what that was. My name tag was more of a statement than a name; it was different. This should have been a great opportunity to provide benefit and value statements to those who asked the question, prompting more information and potential sales. That would have been ideal, but just like 87% of the attendees, I was not prepared to answer that question. So I just said, "It is an event for women" and they responded, "Oh, okay" and walked off. WOW! Did that grab their interest? Can you feel the rushing wind of all those people running to buy a ticket? That is when I started to realize you only have three seconds to stand out and grab your potential customer by the heart and throat. Not literally, of course, but with his perceived value, benefits, results, and solutions. Especially if you have been clever enough to have them ask you what you do or get them interested in your product or service.

CHAPTER 2

The Language of Client

A client stated the following during an interview:

> "I often speak with different business owners at networking events and ask them what they do. They usually answer with their professions - doctor, real estate agent, or accountant—or they take several minutes to explain their businesses. Afterwards, I still do not know what they do and all they have accomplished is to confuse me more. Frankly, if I don't understand what it is you do, how can I know if I need what your business offers or refer you to someone who might?"

Many of the clients we interviewed stated that when they ask "What do you do?" they are really asking if the person has a product or service they could use, refer someone to, or align themselves with. The average answer they received, however, was confusing or unclear to them. Sometimes the person was so focused on explaining all the features of her business that the listeners lost all future interest in the business.

"When people ask what do you do, they are not asking you for your profession, they are asking what your business can do for them."

JOE PICI

Perceived Value

Much has changed in the business world today and how customers decide on what to buy. Clients today are inundated with information, marketing and commercials that sound like white noise or static. A recent study showed that one New York Sunday Times newspaper contained more information that an eighteen-century man learned in their entire lifetime. It is imperative to speak benefits, results, and solutions from the customer's point of view in order to break through the noise and stand out for the client to take notice. Therein lies the main challenge most business owners have on how to speak Client. How do you clearly communicate the value of your products or services to the customer so he pays attention and buys? As you become versed in the language of Client, you will be able to do just that. This is the only way you will stand out.

"Language is the dress of thought."

SAMUEL JOHNSON

The "what is in it for me?" question is not a new epiphany in marketing or sales. It is one that has been forgotten, buried in the emotional brandings of "got to have it" and "look at me, I am in the popular group" mindset of the last ten years. This was dictated and driven by mega companies and ingenious, expensive super bowl marketing campaigns. They decided what was in fashion, what was "cool," and where the trends were.

As people's finances tightened, the market became more self-reliant and focused on survival, not on what everyone else thought. Think about those who did not have any money and suddenly won a windfall. How did they act when they won the money versus when they did not have it? The more money, the more the need to impress and compete; the less money, the higher the need for self-preservation. (At the time this book was written 2010, most major brands have opted to use social media as the chosen form of advertising during the super bowl. These well known brands stated they wanted to connect with their audience in their language in order to provide a better and more realistic experience).

In this day and age the average consumer no longer perceives ***value*** as a brand, but the benefit or solution it can provide to her current situation. Solve her pain and your perceived value rises to the top. Have you ever gone to the grocery store and needed to buy a bar of soap? You did not care about the brand, you just needed soap. Then you find the aisle and there are 40 different kinds of soap.

You begin to read about the different kinds and you find some appealing, so you keep looking. Next thing you know you have spent 30 minutes looking at soap. Now that you have seen all the different options soap can offer you, your perceived value of soap has now changed, and unless you find a bar of soap that provides you with unique solutions or benefits for your new needs, you may never leave the aisle.

You finally find one that stands out; it moisturizes and leaves you with a clean scent. Now you have decided you want smoother skin and an "Irish" clean. This soap is the only one that does that but it costs $1.50 more than the others. You buy it anyway.

The basic elements of soap are the same; the results and the pain they solve are unique. This increases the perceived value. This soap solved the need you had and it was the only one that could. So it was worth paying the extra $1.50. That is *perceived value!*

The purpose of perceived value is to build a higher expectation for the client and communicate the solution to her needs. The value of your product or service is presented in such a way that the client can see the benefit to her business or person.

The lack of this perceived value can be seen at many leads groups or networking events. The intent, in most groups, is to stand up and give a thirty-second to one-minute description of your business or service in order to educate the attendees on how to provide you with quality referrals. What you will hear is the equivalent of the aisle full of soap. Initially, the presentations look and sound the same—all features and no perceived value to the listener.

The problem is that the listeners also have to stand up and talk. Speaking in public is one of people's biggest fears. They would rather burn alive than give a presentation to others. And not only are the listeners hearing an avalanche of features that sound the same, they are rehearsing in their minds what they are going to say without their voices cracking or having a mental cramp.

To make an impact, you have to shake them out of their fear coma and hit them between the eyes. Stand out like the soap with the "Irish clean." Have you ever shocked someone with static buildup? It gets their attention. You must do the same and the only way to do that is to provide benefits, results, and solutions in the client's perspective.

Customers just want one simple question answered,

"What is in it for me?"

So how do you answer that question clearly? By asking yourself some questions of your own:

1. What does my client really need?
2. What is my client struggling with?
3. What are three solutions or benefits that my product provides to my client?
4. How can I add more value than my clients expect?

Features vs. Benefits

When we asked businesses about their benefits, most of the answers we heard were features or characteristics of their products or services.

Some of these "benefits" were:

- "Our organic juice tastes really good."
- "My lip balm is small and compact."
- "It has twenty fruits and vegetables."
- "This is xyz brand. It is the very best on the market."

These are all features and characteristics of the product or service, not the benefits it provides. This is where the confusion lies. The business owner tends to think of how the client uses the product or service while the client is trying to decide why he needs it in the first place. If price was ever an issue for your product or service, this is why. Features create price comparisons. Benefits, results, and solutions create value. When creating a logical desire to purchase, price is no longer an issue. This is when the client sees the benefits of the features the product provides, not what it costs.

Amateurs speak features, characteristics, or product names. Professionals speak benefits, solutions, and results. A professional selling his product or service would sound more like:

- Would you like to know how to increase your energy without crashing afterward?
- I help women slow down the aging process.
- We help realtors in a down market create ongoing referrals.
- "If I could show you a way to earn extra income on a part-time basis, would that be worth 15 minutes of your time?

"Features create price comparisons.
Benefits, results, and solutions create value."

RICO PEÑA

This is the language of Client; it grabs your attention and creates a desire and genuine interest for more information about the product or service.

Your Target Audience

It is, of course, a lot easier if you know who your specific citizen is within ***the Client Nation.*** This is the individual client that wants and needs your business. That means understanding the industry you want to play in as well as the individual client interested in your business. If all you had to do was to market and sell to one person, how much easier would your life be? And how much more profitable would your business be?

Sara Blakley is a great example of this. She is the creator of SPANX form-fitting pantyhose and undergarments that are now a world phenomenon.

Here is her story:

> **I never dreamed visible panty lines and uncomfortable thongs would inspire me to become an inventor.**
>
> "Like so many women, I bought clothes that looked amazing in a magazine or on the hanger, but in reality magnified every panty line and imperfection — clothes that eventually made their way to the 'maybe one day I'll be flawless' section of my closet where they remained unworn.
>
> With $5,000 in savings out of the back of my apartment, a whole lot of Internet research, patent writing, cold-calling, less-than-shy demonstrations for buyers, and a call from Oprah . . . Spanx was born!"
>
> SARA BLAKLEY

Sara focused on one type of client and solved very specific issues for that market—women **(the specific client)** who worried about panty lines and uncomfortable thongs **(the issue or pain)**.

Professional business owners will research and study the customer in every way to get to know her better and know her pain. They find out what the customer's needs are and create a convenient way to provide the solution to the client at an affordable price. This way, when they are ready to approach the individual, they do so with confidence and a high level of expectation. The customer will buy the product or service or refer someone who will; the business owners already know what the client's pain is and have a solution for it.

This is primarily how focus groups work. They have one particular product and ask a target market their opinions on a laundry list of questions. This helps the company provide exactly what the market wants.

The more focused and narrow your market, the bigger the results. Expenses will be less and your perceived value will increase, as well as your profits, because you are solving the needs of that particular market. Individuals who have this knowledge and understanding of their clients are the ones who flourish at networking events, leads groups, and direct market companies. They only focus on the type of client that fits the needs that their products can solve. This makes the event less stressful and more profitable.

"There are two kinds of knowledge. One is general, the other is specialized. General knowledge . . . is but of little use in the accumulation of money."

NAPOLEON HILL

Think about your last purchase. Why did you buy that particular item or service? What separated it from the competition? What caused you to want or need that item or service? Would you recommend that product or service? Why or why not? Once you can answer these questions honestly, you begin to understand the language of Client and the client's perception. Here is an example.

My wife desperately wanted one of those fancy single-serving coffee machines. Although we had bought a new coffee maker a little less than a year ago, she still wanted another one. Why? Because her best friend, Sue, just got a fancy one and recommended it. Sue talked about how quick and convenient the machine was, the amazing taste of the coffee, and all the flavors you could buy. My wife's logical reason to get a new coffee maker was that the current one leaked occasionally and she could take it to her office and replace the horrible office coffee. Her friend's referral carried a lot of weight. Enough so, that this once acceptable product (our current coffee maker) was no longer good enough, which further increased the perceived value of the new one.

Narrowing your expertise and focusing on understanding the specific client's language could have the same results for your product or service. In my wife's case it was a new coffee maker and her friend's recommendation that created the perceived value. Her language was "who else is using it?" The answer was her best friend.

"The more focused and narrow your market,

the bigger the results and profits."

Mindset

Have you ever been to a country where you did not speak the language? Felt awkward, didn't it? Especially when you begin to raise your voice, hoping the volume actually helps with the translation. Or my favorite situation—playing charades to find out where the bathroom is. This could make what seemed a fun and adventurous trip to a foreign land a stressed and frustrating ordeal because of the inability to communicate even the basic necessities. I witnessed this firsthand.

I took my wife to Costa Rica one summer on vacation. She was eager to practice her three years of high school Spanish with the locals. She approached a guard and asked him a question in Spanish. He simply smiled with no answer, so she did what we all normally tend to do. She asked the same question, only LOUDER. This time she merely got his nervous laughter. My wife again asked the same question and added hand signs, a la charades. Still, the guard just laughed nervously and began looking around for the candid camera. Since she was out of earshot, I moved closer to hear what she was asking. She said, "Donde está el BURRO?" Loosely translated this means, "Where is the DONKEY?" rather than "Donde está el BAÑO?" which means, "Where is the BATHROOM?" One word made all the difference in connecting her needs (the use of a bathroom) with the solution (the location of the nearest bathroom). The guard wanted to help but could not understand my wife's needs; my wife wanted a bathroom but could not communicate what she wanted. Due to the lack of understanding neither one could achieve the desired results.

In the beginning, "speaking Client" is similar to my wife's Costa Rican blunder. We are fluent in the language when we are the customers, however, we tend to struggle with it when we are selling our products or services. So, what do we do? We throw out as much information as we can in the hopes that something will grab our customers' attention. It's like carpet bombing a farm with a 200-pound bomb to get rid of an anthill. It may get the job done but at what expense? In order to speak fluent Client we must first understand what our products or services can do for the client from his perception.

This is the equivalent of Spanish 101: Hola = Hello. Before you can understand the client's perception, you must first understand your own mindset as it relates to your business and clients. This is the primary driver to how you approach, describe, or sell your product or service to the client. Most importantly, the nonverbal cues you provide, created by your mindset, are the very first form of communication your client will experience.

P.S. For those of you who were wondering, my wife did make it to the bathroom...just barely.

You Wear What You Think

Studies have shown that most of our opinions about other people are formed in the first 3 to 10 seconds we meet someone through nonverbal cues.

The following items are what client's told us they see when you approach them:

- Your emotions are on your face: anger, sadness, happiness, cockiness, defiance, joy, or excitement. Your expressions tell me if you love life and what you do, or if you are desperate and just love the money you can make from me.
- Your body can speak as loudly as any bullhorn or announcer. What you don't say may be the very reason I do or don't buy. It can say self-respect by the way you dress –carefully, neatly, and cleanly. Or it can say rebellion with nose rings and other piercings that create your individual image.
- Flamboyance and loud colors state clearly that you are unafraid of my opinion.
- These nonverbal images create the initial perception that your words either support or betray. When you speak more than you listen, I can hear your desperation and the true purpose of your needs.

- When you ask questions, I believe you are interested in me. When you do not ask questions, I assume you are not. When you speak with passion and honesty, I am caught up in your vision. When you complain about things, I can feel your resentment. The experience of your nonverbal cues combined with the words you speak influence me when I am deciding whether or not to buy from you, especially if they are not in sync.

Some people are wearing passion while others are wearing their own personal hell. It all begins with your mindset when you approach any prospect.

The Proverbial Fork in the Road

When we start a business, we do so with high expectations, energy, and enthusiasm. We then tend to realize how much we don't know about running a business. We begin to wear all kinds of foreign hats—CEO, CFO, COO, accountant, sales manager, account manager, PR manager, secretary, delivery guy, janitor, and much more—not including the things we do in our daily lives.

The weight of all these hats greatly affects how we sell and promote our businesses. There are two mindsets in business—SURVIVAL and SERVANT—the proverbial fork in the road.

Understanding the difference between these two mindsets is the first phase of learning to speak Client and doing business successfully with ***the Client Nation***.

"Minds are like parachutes.
They only function when they are open."

JAMES DEWAR

Survival Mode

Once you start your business, you need cash flow like a drowning person needs oxygen. How do you get cash flow? You get it by selling your product or service. You have cash flow to keep running your business and for certain obligations—family, home, insurance, food, and utilities. These depend on the profit your business creates. Your cash flow maintains the overhead you create in order to provide the product or service that generates the profits. But if the overhead is greater than the cash flow, what mindset would you say you are in when you attend a network meeting or meet a new prospect?

If your mindset is in survival mode, you may have the kind of demeanor that says:

- I have to make a sale, the rent is due
- My car payment is coming up next week; I have to get new customers
- College tuition is due; I have to sell something to someone
- I have so much invested in this business
- I have to make it work
- I will prove everyone wrong
- I must sell to survive . . . buy my product, use my service. Pleeeeeeeaseeeeeeee!!!!!!!!!!"

Do any of these sound familiar?

"Your cash flow maintains the overhead it creates in order to provide the product or service that generates the profits."

It would be completely natural to feel that way and it is the primary reason most products or services don't sell. How do you really know if you are in survival mode? The answer is determined by how confident you are about how your product or service will serve the client. When people are confident in their words, they are more interested in the client's understanding of them and less interested in how they will appear to the client. Let's say a single man walks into a club hoping to meet a woman. If he is confident in himself then he will focus on what the women in the club look like. If he considers himself not so attractive and lacks confidence, then he will be more concerned with how he appears to them. Because he is unsure of the reaction of the women he might approach, he will act from a survival mode.

"Hunger, love, pain, fear are some of those inner forces which rule the individual's instinct for self preservation."

ALBERT EINSTEIN

There are two reasons the survival mindset will sabotage any potential to sell your product or service.

REASON #1:

The inability to hear opportunity in the customers' pains or needs.

Because you are so focused on making money at any cost in order to survive, you have it in your mind that you *must* sell something. Your ability to listen becomes fractured. You know if you can just pitch the customer your speech, she will buy. But when you make decisions based on financial distress, the outcome usually causes more stress.

The more stress, the lower the production.

The lower the production, the lower the sales.

The lower the sales, the less cash flow you make.

The less cash flow, the higher the overhead.

The higher the overhead, the lower the profit.

The lower the profit, the higher the stress . . . and the cycle continues all over again.

"Stress is when you wake up screaming and realize you haven't fallen asleep yet."

ANONYMOUS

"Treat your client as a partner in the buying process, rather than a passive subject."

RICO PEÑA

REASON #2:

Bad emotional posture = Desperation

Have you ever met a confident salesperson? He has a demeanor that is approachable and that says, "I can help you. Let me know how I can be of service." It makes you want to know more about him and his product. He seems to know exactly what your pain is and provides a solution for it, without even thinking about it. He listens and creates what seems a tailored solution for whatever you need. When you have bad emotional posture, your clients can feel, see, and smell the desperation. My mentor, Joe Pici, one of the best behavioral sales specialists, once told me, "You can't lead those you need." Think about it. If the survival of your business that month is dependent on one sale or one employee, then your decision and posture will be different than if you did not need that to survive.

Imagine if you had financial security, plenty of cash flow, high profits, low overhead, and you were speaking to a client about your business. How different would your mindset and posture be at that moment compared to "This sale could keep my home from going into foreclosure" or "I could pay some of my creditors with this sale" or "I could survive one more month." Would you say your mindset might be different? Our research shows that those who appeared confident and knowledgeable about their products and client base sold more than the ones who tried to pressure the unsuspecting client.

In the Survival mindset, we tend to believe that *I have to sell no matter what!* The client's needs or perceptions are not the focus in that thought; surviving is. So we keep pushing and saying the same thing repeatedly to everyone we meet. We think, "It will work this time" and get frustrated when it does not work, without understanding why. The definition of insanity is doing the same thing over and over again, expecting a different result. Our body language is forceful, pushy, defensive and even worse, it reeks of desperation. Would you buy any product or service from a desperate person?

I think of that guy in the trench coat standing on the corner who says, *"PSSSST what do you need? I got anything you need. Everything is cheap!"* Then he opens his trench coat and you see watches, chains, purses, shoes, and umbrellas. He is doing everything he can to sell you something. And he is willing to say or do anything to make a sale. Which is easier: selling to clients who want your product or service or trying to convince clients why they should buy?

"Long-term clients come from the people who want your product or service, not from those you have to convince."

RICO PEÑA

Many sales have been lost because the salesperson knew what the customer needed even if the client did not, and proceeded to tell the client as much. How many times have you ignored or not heard what the customer was saying because you were talking in your head, waiting to pitch your well-rehearsed presentation? I know I have done that and I always lost the sale.

Financial strain or prosperity can directly affect how you treat your business, yourself and, most importantly, your customers.

"The definition of insanity is doing the same thing over and over again, expecting a different result."

During one of our client shopping interviews, a client told us this story:

"I had been searching for a pair of jeans I saw in a magazine. I visited all of the department stores that carried jeans with no success. Several weeks later a jean specialty store opened not far from my home, I was very excited. I went to the store and it was beautiful. They had every jean imaginable and then some. After about 20 minutes, I could not find the jeans I was looking for. I looked around and could not find a clerk or salesperson anywhere.

Finally I found a salesperson in the office looking over some paperwork. She seemed very stressed. I politely asked her if she carried the type of jeans I was looking for. She seemed annoyed that I interrupted her and pointed at a stack of jeans on the table. I searched and found my size.

I went to the dressing room to try them on and the door was locked. I asked the salesperson if she would unlock the door so I could try on the jeans. She did, obviously not too happy to have to get up. I tried them on and they fit perfectly in all the right places. I looked at the price tag. With the coupon they were a bargain.

After I tried on several different pairs, I decided on the

> ones I wanted and once again approached the salesperson to let her know I was ready to check out. She stated in a very rude and dismissive way that she would be there in a moment. Ten minutes and six clients waiting in line later, there was still no salesperson. All we could hear was the salesperson yelling on the phone. I left the jeans on the table and walked out.
>
> I was very disappointed and sad that anyone would treat clients that way. I later found out that the salesperson was the owner. I made sure to tell all my friends about my experience at that store. It has since closed down."

I asked this client why she did not buy the jeans anyway. She had been looking for them for a while, they fit well, and they were on sale.

She said, "I could not buy them because every time I wore them, they would remind me of the horrible experience I had when purchasing them."

By not serving the client, the owner cost her business many potential clients and, worst of all, the disservice created the type of publicity no business wants, the negative kind. This client blasted her bad experience to all her friends both in person and through all her social media networks. Eventually the store went out of business. This is the power of the World of MouthOnomics. What are your clients saying about your business? What experience are you providing?

"The perception your client receives
from the experience you provide
will be exactly what the client will share with others."

RICO PEÑA

Servant Mindset

> *"Your true worth is determined by how much more you give in value than you take in payment."*
>
> FROM THE BOOK *GO GIVERS*

The above quotation is the essence of having a servant's mindset. But how do you get there?

The servant's mindset comes from the heart. That is when we serve our customers not just for profit but because we want to, unselfishly, in order to make a difference in their quality of life.

The story of Johnny the bagger:

In a small town most of us may have never heard of lives a 19-year-old named Johnny who has Down Syndrome and works as a bagger in a small grocery store. Johnny was not unlike many of the baggers we have all seen at many other grocery stores. Yet his servant's mindset changed a whole town. The grocery store was facing some difficult times with sales and retaining client loyalty. A marketing expert came in to look for ways to increase traffic and maintain client loyalty. The expert said, "Everyone here can make a difference. Think about something you can do for your customers to make them feel special—a memory that will make them come back." Johnny took this to heart and decided to create something he could give the clients as he bagged their groceries. He created the "thought of the day," a simple saying that would inspire hope and happiness. With the help of his dad, Johnny set up a computer and printed multiple copies of these sayings, then cut them apart and signed the back of each one. As Johnny bagged the customers' groceries he dropped in his thought of the day to say "Thank you for shopping with us."

After one month the grocery store manager was making the rounds in the grocery and saw that Johnny's line was very long while all the other checkout lanes were empty. When he asked the waiting customers if they would like to go to an open cashier they said, "No, thank you. I have to get my thought of the day from Johnny." Some customers even stated that they used to come in once a week but now they try to come in every day to get Johnny's thought of the day. (Story provided by Barbara Glanz. See You Tube video: Johnny the bagger)

A simple unselfish act transformed a troubled store into a place to come experience memories with a staff that serves their clients beyond their expectations. Traffic increased, sales rose, and client loyalty soared. And three months later customers are bringing their friends and co-workers to experience Johnny's thought of the day.

Having a servant's mindset means to genuinely give your clients even more than they expect even if you receive nothing in return. Now some of you might be saying, "If I give more than I receive, how will I survive?" That is a very valid question. Providing more value than the customers expect creates more word of mouth, which creates smiles, which creates less stress. Less stress equals more productivity.

More productivity equals more profit.

More profit equals more confidence.

More confidence equals more sales.

More sales equals more cash flow.

More cash flow equals lower overhead.

Lower overhead equals better value.

Better value equals more repeat clients that refer you, which creates more smiles. And the cycle continues.

Having a servant's mindset creates that atmosphere of productivity and less stress. It may sound a bit far-fetched and may be even against most traditional business practices. But the one common denominator that determines the success or failure of any business is the CLIENT. If you serve your clients and provide them with an experience above and beyond their expectations they will serve you back.

Look back at the story of Johnny the bagger. He did not expect anything in return. He wasn't hoping for notoriety, bigger tips, or even a promotion. He just simply and unselfishly did his part to add value to a seemingly unimportant role by including a little saying that made a difference and improved the experience for many customers. The customers appreciated this random act of kindness that they returned every day to receive their thought of the day.

It does not take much to make a difference, just a passion to do so. Those who had a passion for what they were giving rather than for what they were getting have created the great fortunes in the world. The story of Johnny the bagger teaches us that. If we unselfishly do more for others, as Johnny did, we will have more than enough for ourselves.

Most businesses that survive, regardless of economic times, do so because they go out of their way to find what their clients' needs are and provide them in a convenient and affordable way. Fast food restaurants have this down to a science—drive-through with affordable food you can grab and go. It is convenient and solves the time issues for many commuters. These restaurants provide their customers the personal touch they desire. Their business model always begins with, "How may I serve you?"

"We have to be willing to do more for others in order to have enough for ourselves."

RICO PEÑA

One of my favorite stores is Nordstrom. They have exceptional clothes and amazing customer service. A year ago I purchased a suit from them. While wearing the suit, I tore a hole in the jacket when it got caught on a chair. I took it back to Nordstrom to see what it would cost to repair. The salesperson knew my name. He took a look at the jacket and had the tailor work on it right then. When it was done, it looked brand new. When I asked how much I owed, he said "Nothing. It is a service we provide for our loyal customers." WOW! I purchased another suit, custom shirt, and cuff links that day and I made sure to tell everyone about the amazing service. Did I tell you how great their service was? It was beyond my expectations. This is the place to buy a suit. Have I told you about Nordstrom's customer service?

"Selling is like a seven course meal—small, unique experiences that build on each other and provide an overwhelming experience that the client cannot wait to repeat and share with others."

RICO PEÑA

Think of the businesses or products you are loyal to and would not abandon for any other brand or company. Why is that? What did they do to earn your loyalty in such a way? What could you do to earn that same kind of loyalty from your clients?

Those who can understand the language of Client can determine and anticipate the needs of the client and be able to clearly provide the benefit or solution to the client beyond his expectation.

The servant mindset allows you to naturally listen to the people you are speaking to and hear their needs and the potential opportunities they provide. The survival mindset must sell to *survive.* A servant's mindset sells to *provide.*

My company, Sensational You, focuses on training professional businesswomen and direct marketing groups. We created a business development school called "Sensational You University." Our mission is to empower businesswomen in businesses by creating, connecting, and communicating with powerful alliances in the group. Our events are skill-based trainings and mastermind groups that our participants can use to bounce ideas off the other participants and clients. This creates clarity and real world applications that generate powerful results.

During my one of the events, I began to see two important issues that needed to be addressed.

1. The inability to see the client's perception.
2. The inability to clearly communicate the value and/or solution that the product or service provides for the client.

These two problems seemed to always stop the sale of any product or service. The issue was not the product or service. The challenge was how to communicate the benefits of the product or service to the client in order to create a sale.

This always came back to the client's perception of the product or service as a benefit or solution rather than the company's perception of the features as a reason for the client to buy it. There is a greater return on investment when we listen to the client's needs and provide service that goes beyond expectations.

When I was a mortgage broker, this rule was imperative for survival. Providing customer service that was beyond the customer's expectations meant referrals and future return business. I once had an older customer with limited mobility, who owned a large construction company. I had done my research and determined that if he consolidated all his projects on a new construction loan, he could save 17% on his current interest payments. 17% may not sound like much, but when you are talking millions of dollars it is significant.

I went to his work site and presented him with the proposal. I asked him, "If I could save you 17% on interest payments on all your projects without you having to do anything differently, would that be worth 15 minutes of your time?" He looked at me and said, "Sure." He reviewed all the information and agreed to the deal. I did all the paper work, all the research, and made all the calls to the other banks to handle the money transfers and homeowners insurance. Then I drove two hours one way to his house for him to sign. I did everything that had to be done. Even on the day of the closing, I had the closing attorney go to his home. During all this time, I got to know him and develop a relationship.

When the closing was done, I brought him a bottle of his favorite scotch and a box of his favorite cigars. He thanked me and told me that in his 25 years in business, he had never had such an effortless transaction and exceptional customer service. He referred 18 new customers that year. Every time he would sell a house, I was his preferred lender. I provided every client with the same service.

Take Your Mindset Temperature

So, how do you know if you are in a survival or servant mindset? There is a simple way to make this determination. First, you must take an honest assessment of both your personal and business needs. Take a moment and rethink the last time you were in front of a potential client. Use the quick survey below to determine where you are today. Check all the boxes that apply to you, and then total them up (each check equals one point) at the end. Compare your score to the answer key to see if you are in a survival or servant mindset or somewhere in between. The key to this exercise is to be honest.

Business

- ❏ Were you anxious to talk about and describe your product or service to the client before he could speak?
- ❏ Did you keep interrupting the client when you saw a potential opportunity to plug your business?
- ❏ Can you recall what the client said he needed or wanted at the time?
- ❏ Did you lose interest when you realized the client was not ready to purchase at that moment?
- ❏ Did you begin searching the room for another prospect because you had a certain number of quality prospects you had set for yourself to talk to in order to make the event seem worthwhile?
- ❏ Were you willing to lose profits just to have a sale?
- ❏ Are you frustrated because prospects don't seem to understand how your product or service could benefit them, no matter how you explain it?

Personal

- ❏ Are you constantly thinking about how much you need to make to reduce financial stress?
- ❏ Are you losing sleep because you are not sure how you are going to make ends meet?
- ❏ Do you feel that you may be in over your head?
- ❏ Is what you were originally excited about when you started

your business no longer what drives you to do more?

- ❑ Are you considering finding a job?
- ❑ Are you starting to believe what everyone around you is telling you about your business being a dead end?
- ❑ Are you thinking that if you had more money everything would work out?
- ❑ Is your focus on how you will make it through versus how you can provide a better product or service to your client?
- ❑ Are you promising more than you know you could deliver but hoped you could make it work just to get the sale?
- ❑ Are you refusing to see other options because you want to prove everyone wrong?

Answer key:

0-5 = Servant mindset. Excellent. Keep providing your clients the same kind of service and they will be loyal advocates of your business.

6-11 = Chaos. Stop, drop, and roll. You're on the border of servant mindset and survival. Take a step back and review who your loyal clients are, who constantly buys from you and why. Begin to focus on finding more of those clients and applying the reason why. Talk to your clients and find out what more you could do for them, including the ones that did not buy from you. Seek executive coaching from an expert in your business or from someone who can help you get organized and create a clear path and objectives for your business. Take a look at your business and determine if there are some areas you could outsource in order to give you more time to do the things in which you excel.

12 or higher = Survival mode. Danger zone. Study the following section "In Business for Client." This will help you to define your perfect individual client and regroup to provide the benefits, solutions, or results for that specific client. Identify your return clients and ask them what they would like to see. Survey your one-time clients and ask them what changes they would like to see. Take a closer look at your marketing and who is actually coming in to buy. Look at how you can improve the buying experience for your clients and narrow the client base—who has purchased from you and why—then focus on that type of customer only. Seek executive coaching from a successful individual in your field or business or a person who can assist you to get organized and structured. Keep reading. In the next chapters, you will find out how to better connect and build rapport with clients who will then become your advocates and create new cash flow.

In Business for the Client

Many businesses believe they are in business to sell a product or service. But inanimate objects don't sell themselves. It always takes two individuals interacting in order for a product or service to sell. I believe that you are "in business for the client" to provide an experience that makes the client feel comfortable enough to buy from you and refer you. Your clients determine whether or not you succeed. That is the hidden reality of ***the Client Nation***. Those who embrace this philosophy will be extremely successful. Those who ignore it will suffer its wrath.

Once you have an honest assessment of your business and personal mindset, it's time to re-establish the passion and heart of why you began your business or job in the first place. Something compelled you to do what you are doing. But the passion got lost somewhere under the weight of all the hats you had to wear in order to run the business for the service or product you so much desired to provide. That passion is the flame of desire that will keep you motivated through all your challenges and it is the very first thing a client sees when you speak about your business.

Having a servant mindset creates a cycle of cash flow that allows your business to grow with little to no effort. This is how it works:

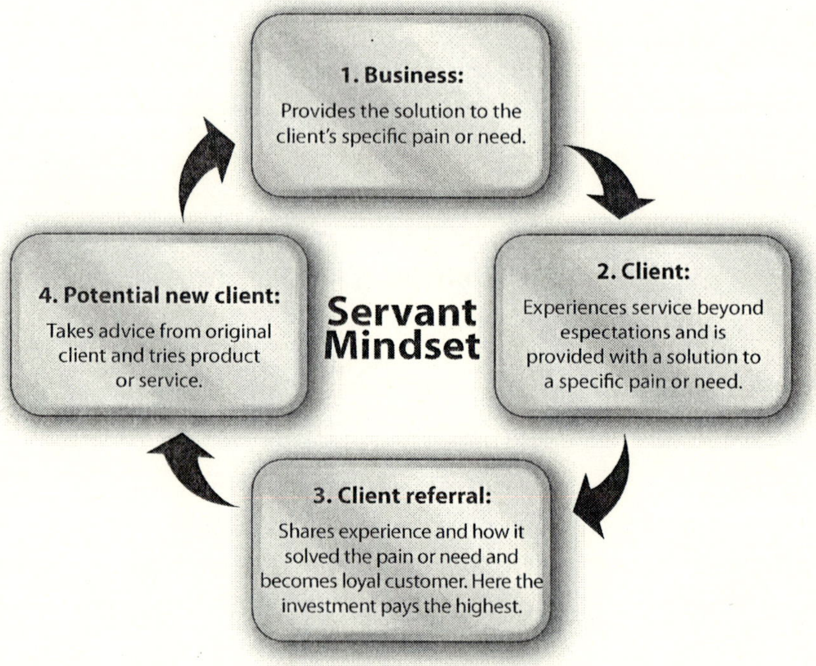

Business provides solutions to the client in his perception coupled with service that is beyond his expectations.

1. Client experiences both great service and solution to problem. He is now happy and satisfied.
2. Client shares these experiences with others, enthusiastically, becoming an advocate for your business.
3. New prospect is eager to experience what the original client described as great service and a convenient and perfect solution to the problem.

This creates a cycle of loyal clients that will become your advocates and business constantly walking through your door.

No matter where your business is, if you make serving your client's needs through his perception the fundamental philosophy of your business, you can expect to stand way above your competition. More importantly, his personal value of your business will soar.

"Price is what you pay.
Value is what you get."

TONY JEARY

"We make a living by what we get,
but we make a life by what we give."

WINSTON CHURCHILL

CASE STUDY

A friend of mine opened a beautiful upscale spa that provided everything a woman could want. He spared no expense, bringing in some of the best hairdressers from New York, professional masseurs, and techniques and products from around the world. The building looked like a home with a view of the Mediterranean ocean, like something you would find in a luxury hotel in Las Vegas or Europe. He built it near high-end homes and neighborhoods. His desire was to bring that kind of luxury for everyone to enjoy. To do so, he priced all his services very affordably.

Two months after his grand opening, he realized he was not getting the results he expected. He didn't understand why. He had the best of everything and no competition, yet his clientele was driving longer distances to other spas.

When he checked out the competition, he saw that not only were they twice as expensive with fewer amenities, they also had a waiting list. So he increased his prices and changed his marketing to reflect a high-end spa designed for luxury and pampering. Within a short period his client base began to grow and he doubled his profits. People were amazed at the quality of service and amenities provided. Before long he had a long waiting list, including the main client base he wanted to serve—the average customer.

The reason for his success was twofold: perceived value with the best products and prices that created that perception, quality services and, most importantly, his desire to serve his clients the very best. He did this beyond their expectations.

Focus on a specific market that knows your product or service and provide benefits, results, or solutions beyond their expectations. If you do, your business will have a higher perceived value. The client will pay more for it and refer you to others. By taking the time to speak Client while researching and defining your individual client, you will develop a unique relationship with your client. This is when being in business for the client will create a loyal client base that will be an advocate for your business.

Lee Iacocca brought Chrysler Corporation back from inferior workmanship, labor disputes, and bankruptcy. He insisted that, in the end, all business operations can be reduced to three words: People, product and profits. People come first. He said, "Down in their hearts, wise men know the truth. The only way to help yourself is to help others. In this or any business, you succeed best by understanding people and helping them towards fulfilling their dreams."

"The eye sees only what the mind is prepared to comprehend."

HENRI BERGSON

CHAPTER 3

The Clarity of Perception

"It is one of the commonest of mistakes to consider that the limit of our power of perception is also the limit of all there is to perceive."

C.W.LEADBEATER

CASE STUDY

Many years ago when I was honorably discharged from the United States Marine Corps, I became a personal trainer. I had studied and practiced this craft extensively in the military and had a passion to help others find their true hidden selves. I had trained and molded many soldiers in my unit and knew I could do the same in the civilian world. So I got a job as a trainer at a local gym. In order to become a successful trainer you must have a reputation for results and knowledge. You also have to be part psychologist, hairdresser, and parent, at least in the listening sense.

I took a job at the front desk giving tours and checking in members. My thought was if they saw me every day and I was the first person they spoke to during the tour, I might have a chance to build a relationship and possibly get them as a client. Even back then relationships were key.

After three months, I began to obtain clients. I only charged $25 an hour even though the average hourly rate was $65 to

$85 for the established trainers. I was very dedicated to my clients and word began to spread quickly and so did my clientele. Working the front desk did help since the clients recognized me and were willing to give me a try. As time went on, I had more clients than I knew what to do with.

That was when I realized that building relationships could create ongoing cash flow and that not having a target market could create stress. I was working 14 hours a day yet I was not getting anywhere. My clients were complaining and it seemed no matter what I did, they were not losing any weight and getting the results we expected.

I took it personally. I was very frustrated and my reputation took a steep dive. I began to question if I was cut out for this kind of work. It was then a good friend of mine, a well-known trainer, pulled me aside and gave me the best advice. He said, "Raise your prices." I looked at him as if he had just insulted my mom or kicked my dog. "Are you crazy? I have rent to pay, a car payment, bills; I cannot afford to raise my prices I will lose clients." Sound familiar? Survival mindset.

He then explained perceived value. He said the reason my clients were not seeing a change was not because of me, but because they were not fully committed to change. He said, "Your clients are your billboard." My price was cheap enough to attract the kind of clients who wanted to say they had a trainer, justify all their bad habits, and blame me for the lack of results. By raising the price, I would eliminate the tire kickers and the ones not willing to commit to the process. The cost becomes the filter. He also said that by raising my rates I would need fewer clients and still make the same amount of money in half the time. This would allow me time for myself to rest, train, and study so I could give my clients the kind of service that was beyond their expectations.

So I raised my prices to $45 an hour and lost 65% of my clients. But, surprisingly, I was enthusiastic again. I was working with clients who were committed to change. They became my billboard and my reputation exceeded my expectations. They began to refer others who were also committed to the process. The next year I raised my price to $85 an hour and began to attract college athletes and semi-pro wrestlers. I knew I could deliver the results they wanted and more. Six months later I raised my rates to $175 an hour and my niche market changed to volleyball, basketball, and football teams, and semi to professional athletes.

They flocked to me. They saw what I did with other athletes and wanted the same. My personal attention to their needs and tailor-made programs and nutrition surpassed their expectations both for training and individual relationships. And I learned that just building relationships was not enough. Building perceived value and relationships with individuals from a specific target market would create ongoing cash flow and quality referrals. All I had to do was deliver beyond their expected value. I was able to do so because I niched my market, became an expert, and I increased my perceived value.

"Building perceived value with individuals from a specific target market will create ongoing cash flow."

When I retired, I was the fitness director for a large facility and only worked with five clients every three months. I was charging $350 an hour and training many of Atlanta's up and coming athletes in addition to professional baseball and *basketball athletes.*

How does the Client Nation perceive the value of your product or service? What are you doing to increase that perception? Sometimes it is just a matter of walking in your clients' shoes.

"How you first meet the public is how the industry sees you. You can't argue with them. That's their perception."

MERYL STREEP

Walk a Mile in My Shoes

In April 2008, Business Week interviewed Howard Schultz, CEO and creator of Starbucks. He had just retaken the position of CEO after the company's stocks began to decline and lose value and stores began to close. In his interview with Maria Bartiromo, a reporter for CNBC, he shared his strategy to re-establish Starbucks' image and growth. In that strategy Schultz mentioned one of the key points to succeed. He said, "The job of every retailer and merchant is to put yourself in the shoes of the customer and ask yourself: 'Are you exceeding their expectations?' That's what we have to do as a business."

When you stray from the client's perception of your business, you will begin to see decline. Starbucks grew by understanding the client's perception of value and exceeding expectations. This was the Starbucks' philosophy, the core principle by which they built their empire.

Exceeding the expectations of the client begins with understanding the client's perceived value.

According to Wikipedia, "in philosophy, psychology, and cognitive science, *perception* is the process of attaining awareness or understanding of sensory information."

The Oxford English Dictionary defines *perception* as "1) the ability to see, hear, or become aware of something through the senses; 2) the process of perceiving; 3) a way of understanding or interpreting something; 4) intuitive understanding and insight." —ORIGIN Latin, from *percipere* – seize, understand.

What the client perceives is what she believes. Creating the right belief plays to the client's senses—smell, taste, sight, touch, and hearing. Connecting with this belief fills the client's expectations.

Creating perceived value, as ***the Client Nation*** would understand it, starts with these simple questions every client tends to ask:

- How does your product or service benefit me?
- Why should I buy from you and not from your competition?
- What service can expect once I am your customer?

When I was a trainer, my clients needed individualized nutrition on a daily basis in order to get the results and performance in their specific sports. I would create weekly food logs and different menus to allow them to fulfill their fitness goals. I went as far as to take their calls at any time from restaurants where they would read me the menu and I would tell them what to eat and how much. That type of customer service and attention to detail separated me from the competition and increased my perceived value. When you find your clients within ***the Client Nation,*** and take the time to know them, their needs, their passion and their desires you can provide results or benefits that create an opportunity you may not have thought of based on the initial product or service you are providing.

"Exceptional service and attention to detail will separate you from the competition and increase your perceived value."

RICO PEÑA

Emotion to Logic

To successfully connect with any client you must first create small experiences throughout the buying cycle, which generates a positive emotion about your product or service. This compels the client to want to know more and eventually buy. The experience must also exceed the client's expectations. This results in the client having a logical conclusion that buying the product or service was the best thing that could have happened to them. Think about an item you were buying and found out at the register it was discounted. How did you feel? The experience does not end there. The key to cement the client's emotional expectations to return and refer you is the after-sale service. The follow-up could be a handwritten thank you card or a phone call to ensure that expectations were met. This experience tells the client you are truly invested in earning her trust and building a relationship.

"Whatever we expect with confidence becomes our own self-fulfilling prophecy."

BRIAN TRACY

Think about the best experience you recently had at a restaurant you visited. What comes to mind first, the task of getting there or the experience you had? Traditionally, the experience is what you remember. Typically it begins with the host greeting you, then a wonderful ambiance, a great server, amazing food, a breathtaking dessert, and a heart-stopping bill. Yet it was all worth it. Most of us would tell everyone in detail about the wonderful experience.

The opposite could also be true. You have a certain expectation of a restaurant either because of a review you read or a referral from a friend. Several small things go wrong and the first thing you are likely to remember is how those small things ruined the experience. When asked about it you tend to say, "Well, it wasn't bad" or "It was just okay" or "The restaurant was beautiful but the food wasn't great" or "The food was amazing but the service was awful." All of these small experiences create a general idea that influences your opinion.

My wife and I had this experience. We were excited about going to a Mexican restaurant that was highly rated in a food review. We entered and the ambiance was incredible. The wait staff was attentive and the entertainment added a sense of the Mexican Riviera. While waiting for our food, there was a child running wild around the restaurant. He would pass by the table and scream. I thought maybe he had hot sauce in his eye. But no, he was just running wild while his parents drank margaritas and were grateful he was not screaming at them. (After hearing him scream, I can understand why the mother was drinking a pitcher of margaritas!)

Neither the management, nor the wait staff, nor the hostess did anything to calm the child or address the issue. All the other patrons were as annoyed and bothered as we were; yet nothing was done. Even though everything else was great—the food, the drinks, and even the dessert—we will never return because of our terrible experience and lack of action by the management.

*"In the **Client Nation***
the intent is to receive
solutions, results, and benefits
in order to make a logical decision to purchase."

When you stay at a hotel, or use a drive-through, the experience of that moment can determine if you return and what you say about it.

You remember and refer based on experiences you have had, good or bad. This is what creates either enthusiasm or disappointment when describing a product or service. Your clients do the exact same thing. Social media today has taken the client's voice into a whole new level of sharing the good and bad experiences they have. The World of Mouthonomics and what the client shares through it, is as important to your financial survival as your product or service itself.

Have you considered the kind of experience your client receives when she buys your product or service? When was the last time you looked at your business in your client's shoes? Have you tried buying the product, online or in person, from beginning to end? Have you asked a client or has one commented on the buying experience?

Here is a surefire way to determine how your business measures up to your client's perception. Have a friend, relative, or someone who will be honest with you and whose opinion you trust, experience your product or service as a client. If you have a storefront, have this person look at the entrance, the displays, and everything the client sees. If it is web-based, examine the experience on the site from surfing to actual purchase. Have her interact with your staff or call customer service. This will give you a different perception of your business. My favorite is to ask different clients their opinions and what they thought of certain aspects of the process. I especially ask those who do not decide to buy.

In a dating scenario you present your best self, hoping to get the attention of the right person. Then you provide an enjoyable experience so the person likes being with you and wants to continue to do so. You do your best to earn his trust so you might have an ongoing steady relationship. Learning how to speak Client is similar to dating. You connect with emotional triggers to provide your client with the right experience that he can enjoy and remember when he tells others.

We start by understanding how to create a connection. We tend to make decisions based on emotions first, and then support them with logic. Some may argue that all their decisions are logical and void, for the most part, of emotion. But I believe every decision has an emotional element to it; some more than others, but an emotional connection nonetheless.

"If the world were a logical place,
men would ride sidesaddle."

RITA MAE BROWN

For example, there may be many logical reasons to buy a house—investment, tax incentive, location, proximity to work, growing or shrinking family. However, many would not consider it their home until elements are introduced that are connected to them.

Painting a room red may not be logical to some but it sure makes it yours. Hanging pictures or using furniture that has nostalgic meaning creates an emotional attachment that makes it a *home*. On the other extreme, you may have purchased a house for logical reasons, yet how logical would you be if you came home from work and found your home and all your belongings burnt to the ground? Or your home was damaged due to flooding and you just found out that your insurance does not cover flooding? There may be some emotion due to lack of results or solutions rather than logic at that moment.

Buying a car may also have the same emotional implications. You may logically state, "I am buying a car because it is reliable, economical, and is a great price." You may even logically determine how much money you will save by buying an environmentally friendly vehicle. No emotion there, right? Until you walk outside and find a cement truck has backed into your car right before you had to get to a meeting. There might be some emotion then.

No matter how big or small the purchase, there will always be a level of emotion that must be triggered in order to create value. This in turn validates the purchase from a logical perspective. Put simply, every purchase begins with emotion and is validated by logic. This is the introduction to connecting to the client's perception and why we need to learn to speak Client. Each client has an emotional trigger that has a perceived value. Understanding what this is will allow you to provide the comfort zone and language that will allow the client to logically decide to purchase your product or service.

Relational Business

When you learn the language of Client, you begin to see and understand your clients' true needs in their perception. You can then create a comfortable environment and begin to build trust and a relationship. Large corporations spend billions of dollars to build that perceived relationship with their target audience.

- Wendy's – You know her Dad – Dave makes the best hamburger.
- Disney – a man with a mouse and a dream.
- Wal-Mart – great products at a good price.
- Orville Redenbacher – the best popcorn.
- McDonald's – Ronald McDonald and the kid's mealtime fun with a toy in every box.
- Hello I'm a MAC and I am a PC.
- When you are hurt and can't work, who do you need? Aflaaaaac.

Advertisers know we will buy from someone with whom we can identify. They also know we will buy something because it gives us a perceived relationship with someone we admire. For example, Michael Jordan endorses shoes because millions of people see him as their hero or as an encouragement to make their dreams come true.

"I want to be like Michael!"

In order to effectively be successful in ***the Client Nation*** we must understand that people, not products, sell to people. We must begin to build relationships that create a common ground and a level of trust that allows our clients to feel comfortable to do business with us regardless of the economy.

"Relational business begins with building the kind of trust a client can identify with."

I recently visited a men's store in search of cuff links. I have an affinity for cuff links, the more unusual the better. They are a way to express my identity, especially as a speaker. As I walked into the store, a warm and friendly sales staff greeted me. They quickly asked my name and how they could help me. They offered me wine, champagne, anything I wanted. I immediately felt like a VIP. They poured over books, the Internet, and their inventory to find the right cuff links. This was all without any pressure or an up-sell. They took the time to get to know me. They were building rapport. They finally found the cuff links I was searching for, ordered them, and shipped them to my home. For my common language, I like results. If I have a specific need, do not try to up-sell me. They did not.

I received a call following up on the status of my cuff links and when I could expect them. I was told if I was not satisfied to bring them back and they would issue a full refund or, if it were more convenient, they would pay for shipping back to the store. *That* is customer service. *That* is relational business.

For my behavior style, I need to trust you before I will buy from you. I am there to buy, not to shop. There is a big difference. When I buy, it is because I need something to accomplish a task or project. I needed the cuff links to complete my outfit for my presentation. I had a certain image I was creating that would connect with the clients I was presenting to. I go in to get what I need and I am done. Give me results, don't try to B.S. me, and I will begin to trust you. If you provide me with all that plus customer service beyond my expectations, I will refer you. My wife shops because she wants something and enjoys the experience of shopping. That is why some shoppers tend to take an entire day to find one item. It is not about the item. It is about the experience of interacting and finding the item. As you can see, I am not initially interested in small talk. My wife, on the other hand, is. If you do not chat, smile and show interest in what she has to say, she will not like you and therefore not trust you nor will she buy from you. Also, if we are together and I see you are ignoring her, I feel you do not respect her and therefore you do not respect me. No sale. Can you begin to see how connecting to the client in his own pace can begin to increase sales?

Relational business understands people and builds quality connections with others based on their priorities. Building quality connections takes time and practice in addition to knowledge of behaviors, pace, and priorities. These tools will help you develop the relationships that will build a strong foundation for your business in ***the Client Nation.*** By understanding the pace and priority of each individual we meet, we can reduce something as complex as diversity or individual boundaries to a simple language that creates a comfort zone for clear communication, respect and value.

Understanding Human Behavior

Understanding how to communicate and connect with other people is imperative to any long-term success. When you build relationships, behavior is the key word, not personality, because behaviors never lie but personalities can change based on the environment or what the client may be feeling at the moment. Learn to address the behavior of the moment and you will always create a solid connection.

"Behaviors never lie . . .
They adjust."

JOE PICI

Understanding human behavior will allow you to clearly see two critical issues necessary to master the Client dialect:

1. Your own needs, drivers, and blind spots.
2. Your client's needs, drivers, and perceived value.

To skip this fundamental process in the language of Client is to miss the key principle that will allow you to clearly communicate with your client. This is the piece I have found most businesses and direct sales professionals need in order to truly accelerate their success long-term. This piece acts like a translator that enables you to hear and understand your client's common language and to respond quickly and fluently in that language.

Why is this important? As we have discovered, ***the Client Nation's*** perceived value is based on benefits, results, and solutions. These elements are necessary before your clients are willing to buy or refer any business.

In the next chapter we will go more in depth into the different behavioral styles, natural tendencies, and comfort zones found in each of the four regions of ***the Client Nation.*** The challenge most businesses have is how to clearly communicate with their clients. By understanding their behaviors, you will be able to do so quickly.

CHAPTER 4

The Four Regions

Prior to this chapter we took a space view of ***the Client Nation.*** Now we are coming in for a closer aerial view, followed by a laser focus on the clients for each region. This information you are about to experience will provide the missing link to many of the lost sales, slow business, and knowing how to plug into the World of MouthOnomics.

"You are a blend of all behavioral styles."

As you read the descriptions of the regions of ***the Client Nation,*** you will begin to notice that you can identify with some, if not all, of the behavioral styles. There will be, however, one particular region that you tend to identify with the most. This is your common language, what makes you 'tick." In the following chapters, we will take a closer look at what that "tick" is and why it "ticks."

Every region has strengths that make success in sales attainable. It also has blind spots that lose sales and creates bad publicity which speeds through the World of Mouthonomics. The information you're about to experience will teach you how to recognize these attributes in yourself as well as your client.

Joe and Dawn Pici explain in the following chapter, "Becoming Your Best Self" from their book, *Sell Naked on the Phone:*

> "Your search for extraordinary sales skills begins with you: your needs, your fears and your motivations. Every person on this planet needs to have their needs filled. As a sales professional, you are no different.
>
> - Your internal desire to have your needs met creates your behavior.

- Your behavior sends messages to your clients.
- Your client responds to all messages you send: verbal and nonverbal.

> Even if they [your clients] only sense the messages subconsciously and cannot tell you what they pick up from you, their sense of what you are communicating still drives their behaviors. When your behavior communicates that you are not genuine, or are working to meet your own needs, you repel potential clients. When they sense that you are working to meet their needs, they will tend to trust you more and feel a closer connection (at least in a business sense) with you. The resulting trust and connection will lead to more sales."

The information you are about to experience will help you highlight your strengths and needs as well as your blind spots. You will know what to adjust, and see the areas where you need to practice, in order to clearly speak your individual client's common language effectively.

The Comfort Zone

Every behavioral style has different natural tendencies. These tendencies act as "comfort zones"—the areas where people feel most comfortable. By understanding your client's common language you will be able to create a "comfort zone" and adjust your behavior accordingly to connect and communicate more effectively. This will create the kind of relationship that makes your client comfortable to do business with you and become an advocate and a repeat customer.

Natural Tendencies

Everything we do in life, whether we see it or not, involves some form of sales. As children we negotiate (most parents would call it nagging or begging) to get what we want. Take a child to the toy store or the grocery store and he will relentlessly ask, beg, scream, or be annoying until he gets what he wants. Adults call this "guerrilla-style negotiations."

Recently I saw this in action. I was eating lunch at a local restaurant when a mother and her young daughter entered. They looked at the menu on the wall and decided what they wanted. As they approached the counter, the little girl saw these big cookies cleverly placed at a child's line of sight. She asked her mother if she could please have one. Her mother said no and told her to go have a seat. She quickly did and waited for her mother to get up to the register. As her mother got closer, the child went to her and began to ask for the cookie once again. Her mother said no because she was going to bake cookies when she got home. The daughter quickly replied. "That is what you said yesterday. Please!" She knew if her mom paid before agreeing to the cookie she would not get one. So she began to ask every three to four seconds, tugging at her mom's arm. "Please! Please! Mom? Pleeeeaseeee!" After a minute of this her mother agreed. The little girl skipped to the table with a triumphant smile and her big cookie.

We could learn a lot from kids. That is effective guerrilla-style negotiation. As teenagers, we discover the power of selling the benefits to our parents to borrow the car or purchase a cell phone. As adults, we begin to see the power of marketing while in the dating scene and looking for the right mate. At the work place, whether it is a product, service, or promotion, we discover the power of negotiation.

No matter why or how, we are always selling to someone. This, however, is not enough. We've learned through our research that knowledge and techniques were not enough for most salespeople and businesses to be as successful as they should have been. We discovered that the missing link to greater sales correlates with understanding the client's needs and the awareness of the sale person's blind spots.

In other words, in order to connect and clearly speak the common language of your clients, you must identify their behavior and adjust your own to match theirs. This creates a comfort zone based on their natural tendencies where your clients can thrive. This in return increases the perceived value of your product or service and therefore increases your sales.

An Inside Look

In ***the Client Nation*** there are four regions:

The **DOMINANT** region

The **INTERACTIVE** region

The **STEADY** region

The **CALCULATING** region

Each region, as with clients, has different perceptions. During our interviews, we discovered that when we presented all the clients with the same facts, their reactions were based on their perceptions or what region of ***the Client Nation*** they came from.

The **DOMINANT** region wanted to know, *"What is going on here?"*

The **INTERACTIVE** region inquired, *"Who is invited to this function?"*

The **STEADY** region wondered, *"How do we need to do this project?"*

The **CALCULATING** region asked, *"Why are we doing this?"*

The facts of the project are not important. The *perception* of each region was eye-opening and provided insights into how to increase the perceived value of the product or service based on those clients needs.

"All our knowledge has its origins in our perceptions."

LEONARDO DAVINCI

Sadly, very few people focus on this. This is why when you apply and learn the language of Client you will be miles above your competition. If you can learn to identify and communicate in the common language of your clients, which will provide you with their perceptions, your business will accelerate to the speed of life.

Let's take a look at a map of the four regions of The Client Nation.

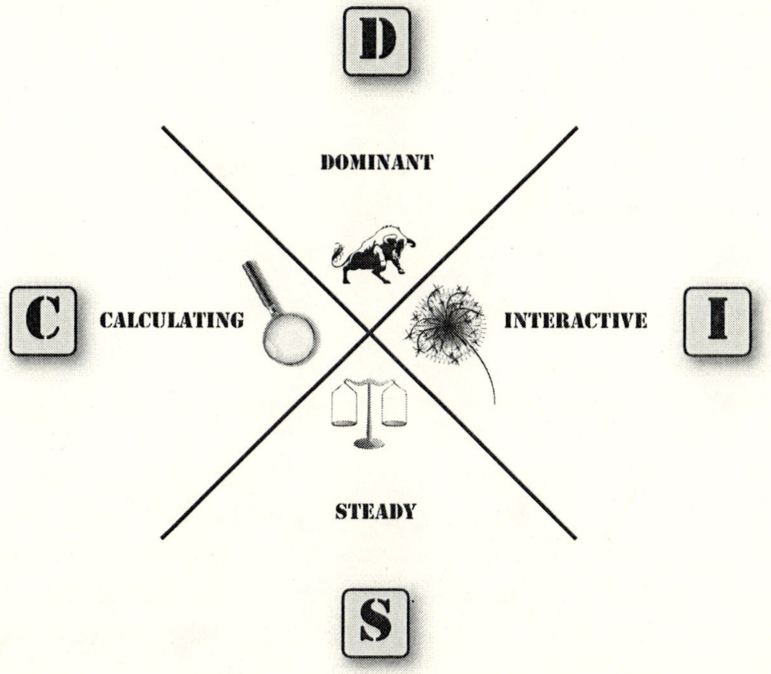

Each region is important in its own unique way. Together they balance each other and when they all work in harmony there is nothing that can keep them from success. As you read through each region think about your team, employees, clients, and even family members. See if you can determine the region they would relate to the most. Which region do you tend to associate with 51% of the time? This will help you begin to identify different clients and their common languages and how they may differ from yours, allowing you to appreciate and comprehend their unique perceptions.

The only way to perfect any language is with practice. But before we can look at the clients individually, it's important to see how they fit as a whole in ***the Client Nation.***

As we mentioned in the previous chapter, we can begin to understand each other's common language by simply understanding the person's perception through his pace and priorities.

The Client's Pace

"If a man does not keep pace with his companions, perhaps it is because he hears a different drummer. Let him step to the music which he hears, however measured or far away."

HENRY DAVID THOREAU

Pace is like that internal rhythm we all tend to live by. The speed in which we are most comfortable, some live for speed, others the security of doing things slowly. It is where we feel at home or where we retreat to when we feel scared or cornered. Pace is where the connection to your clients is made. Though business is not decided at this point, the decision to move forward is. This is where you can begin to create the comfort zone for your clients to decide to buy based on their priorities. The following will provide you with the directions necessary to begin to see and connect with any client's pace.

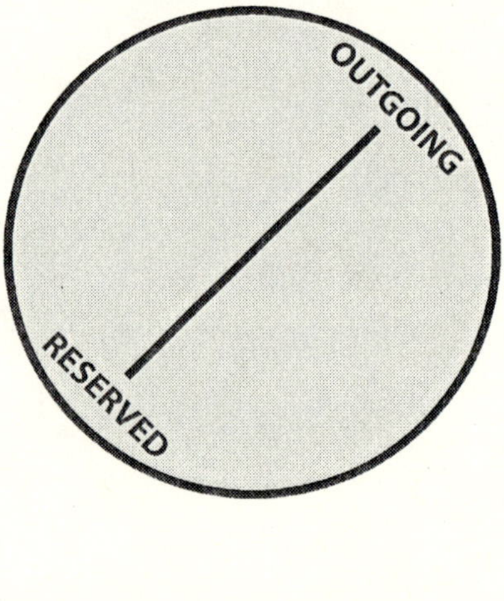

Outgoing

On the top half of ***the Client Nation*** is the outgoing or fast-paced citizen. Just as the name suggests, these clients are fast-paced, autobahn style—slam the accelerator and apologize for it later. This area is energetic. Clients are powerful, driven, impressive, and flashy. The citizens of the outgoing half of ***the Client Nation*** can be described as:

- Optimistic
- Energetic
- Involved
- Decisive
- Enthusiastic
- Always on the move

They live by the word "go." New York City and Las Vegas come to mind when I think of this group.

Reserved

On the lower half of the nation is the complete opposite, the reserved or slow-paced area. You can float and relax here, as if you were on a slow winding river. This group is not in a hurry; clients take their time to do everything. Their movements, thoughts, and decisions are not rushed but thought out carefully and with precision. They are a cautious group and reluctant to get involved in too many activities. The citizens of the lower half of the nation can be described as:

- Cautious
- Concerned
- Reluctant
- Contemplative
- Discerning

They live by the "measure twice and cut once" philosophy. Small Montana towns and the Bayous of New Orleans come to mind when I think of this group.

But We All Speak English, Right?

Even though everyone here in the U.S. speaks English, that does not necessarily mean we can understand each other. For example, if you took a person born and bred in Boston and dropped him in the middle of the bayou in New Orleans, he might have a difficult time communicating with the locals, not to mention avoiding the alligators. The pace or speed of how the locals speak and the dialect they use are unfamiliar to him. The same might happen if you took a surfer from California and dropped him in the middle of the Bronx. He might find it challenging and may even be in shock. Duuuude!

As we mentioned in the Outgoing area, some people move at a faster pace; they act before they think, tend to be more aggressive, always seem to be on the go, and are likely to be outspoken. On the other side of the spectrum in the Reserved area, people tend to move at a slower pace; the term slower pace does not refer to their intelligence level or capabilities, simply the rhythm or speed in which they tend to think and move. This group tends to process and think before they act, they want facts and information, and they seem quiet and reserved. Where are you more comfortable 51% of the time? Do you tend to be faster paced or slower paced? What we have found through our research is that connection starts here. It is also where most sales are lost. If you are a slower-paced person in a store with a fast-paced salesperson talking to you at a million miles per hour and trying to sell you something, you might become a little irritated. Would you buy from someone who irritates you? Can you do business with people who are irritated? Most of the time we are not aware of this difference because this is who we are naturally. That is why it is important to discover where we stand in the connection phase and adapt to our clients' paces to allow them to be comfortable so they will buy. Can a sale move forward without a connection? In most cases, it won't.

Referring back to my personal training story, this was a lesson I had to learn quickly after being in the Marine Corps. In the military, our life depends on reaction, not hesitation. We were expected to be of the same mind and movement with instant obedience to order. This was achieved through intense training and physical and mental endurance, while a drill instructor yelled in our ears to push harder.

This, however, did not translate well into the civilian mindset. Imagine a tennis mom with three kids, a dog, and a minivan trying to lose 10 pounds. My screaming in her face to "Give me 10 more" and "Stop whining" did not have the same effect it did with my recruits. Needless to say, she did not return after our initial session. I think she may still be in therapy!

It was not until later that I learned to connect with my clients in *their language* in order to motivate them and eventually see results. This in turn increased my business, my quality leads, and, above all, my profits.

Being intense can cause a more reserved or slower pace client to think you are in need of decaf or, even worse, angry. But being too laid back may irritate some clients who wish you would "*JUST GET TO THE POINT ALREADY!*" We all act and speak from our own common language or the perception in which we are most comfortable. As with breathing or blinking, we don't think about it, we just do it. We need to reframe our perceptions and begin to see the needs of our clients from their vantage point. Then we can provide them with the solutions they are looking for which in turn will create a comfort zone and an experience they will enjoy and share with others.

It is just like being in that foreign country. After a week of struggling to communicate, you find a storeowner who speaks your language, enough for you to understand each other. At that moment, you may feel relief that someone understands you and can finally assist you with your needs, which improves your experience and your comfort zone. It allows you to know, like, and trust the business, and create a memorable moment you won't forget and will share with others.

Connecting at your client's pace tells the client you care enough about his needs and your relationship with him to go out of your comfort zone to make him comfortable. This begins to create that *beyond expectation* experience that will separate you from the competition and put into motion the positive word of mouth marketing all business owners search for. By doing so, you will increase your business, your loyal customer base, and your ongoing leads.

Application:

List two names of clients that have recently purchased from you and determine what pace they were:

Name:______________________________ (Pace) Fast or Slow

Name:______________________________ (Pace) Fast or Slow

Based on what you have just learned, what would you do differently to connect with each client? ______________________________

____

____

____

The Client's Priorities

"Action expresses priorities."

MAHATMA GANDHI

While pace may be the reason we like or trust someone, our priorities are the reason we decide to purchase a product or service from that person. Each region of ***the Client Nation*** has its own behaviors and temperaments. Priorities inspire the reason WHY the clients of each region buy. These priorities are the primary fuel that drives each citizen to the logical reason to buy any product or service.

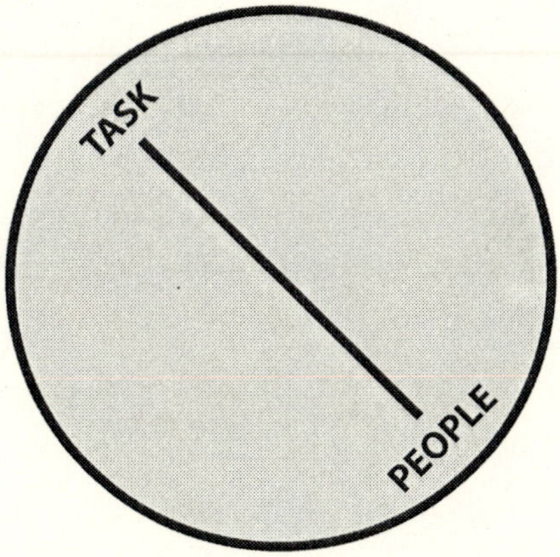

Task

The Task-oriented clients (left side) like to do things, make plans, or work on projects. They strive to have a well-oiled, fine-tuned working machine, whether it is their business or the organization of their garage. They are always striving for perfection. They are extremely competitive and will find a way to win. They are also considered "high tech." They like to have the newest technology and gadget on the market, sometimes for show, but mostly because it helps them get the task done better.

They create checklists and focus on the task at hand. Just like soldiers, they must accomplish the mission at all costs. Their priorities tend to be on accomplishing a project, assignment or job. Some words that define the left side of the nation are:

- Process
- Organization
- Function

- Program
- Plan
- Project

When I think of this group, I always think of a bloodhound tracking a scent. His focus is finding the source of that scent and nothing will distract or stop him from this task. When the Task-oriented people purchase, they go in, get what they want and get out. They need what it is they are buying. Remember, they still have a task to complete and the product or service helps to do that.

People

The People-orientated clients (right side) are the most fun and hospitable in the nation. This is *not* to say that the Task-oriented folks are inhospitable. But their focus is on the tasks they have to accomplish. The people side of the nation loves people; those clients are just wired that way. Their priorities tend to be more about relationships, people and, above all, FUN!

These clients are about talking, feeling, empathy, openness, and sharing one's heart. Their motto is:

"I don't care how much you know.

I want to know how much you care."

Some words that define this group are:

- Feelings

- Relationships
- Caring
- Sharing
- Emotions
- Friendships

I always think of Fourth of July fireworks and cute kittens or puppies when I think of this side of the nation. The feelings they evoke are exactly how they make you feel when you are with them.

The People-oriented clients don't buy - they shop. When you buy, you do so for a particular product or service. That is why Task-clients go in, get what they need, and get out. When you shop for a product or service, you do so for the experience. People-oriented clients shop for the experience of meeting new people and the thrill it provides. They tend to relish the attention of the salespeople and all the new things on display. They are actually purchasing based on the salesperson and the experience. The item or service will remind them of the experience they had.

The experience, whether task-oriented or people-oriented, is directly related to the clients' perception. This, ultimately, will determine for them when to buy your product or service.

Application:

List the name of a client who seemed to be more Task-oriented.

Name a client who seemed to be more People-oriented.

Name:____ Task

Name:____ People

Based on what you have just learned, what would you do differently to sell to each of their priorities?

____

____

Even though *the Client Nation* is so diverse, we can begin to understand each other's common language simply by understanding our client's perceptions through their paces and priorities. This allows us to see our clients beyond the outward appearance and closer to the true nature of who they really are. We may be different in sex, race, nationality, size, or shape, but we can find common ground by identifying and understanding our common language. Learning each other's common language helps us to recognize our perceptions, needs, wants, and motivators. It helps us to connect with others at a deeper level - the level of rapport.

Rapport is the deepest level of business connection you can achieve with your client. With rapport, you become the consultant, the go-to guy, and the advisor. You gain not only a loyal customer who believes in your product or service but a champion who will speak about it to everyone he meets.

WARNING!

Without the true desire to benefit your client through a servant mindset, these approaches will appear false and manipulative from your client's perception and create a perceived value of zero. When you apply these lessons with the intent to build genuine relationships, your effectiveness will increase and so will your perceived value.

Skills require constant practice. Proficiency will not happen overnight, but as you begin to apply these new lessons and see the results, you will find it easier to connect with your client's pace and provide the needed priorities to make a buying decision. This will help you create the comfort zone your client seeks. Soon, this will feel as natural as walking or breathing. Once you have developed and practiced these skills, you will have successfully mastered all four areas of speaking the language of Client fluently.

Recap: We have seen the Outgoing, Reserved, Task, and People sides and their pace and buying priorities. Now let's take an aerial view of these four areas.

The Four Quadrants

We have seen the overall picture of ***the Client Nation*** and its unique paces and priorities that can influence the client's buying decisions. When these are combined, they create the four quadrants of ***the Client Nation.***

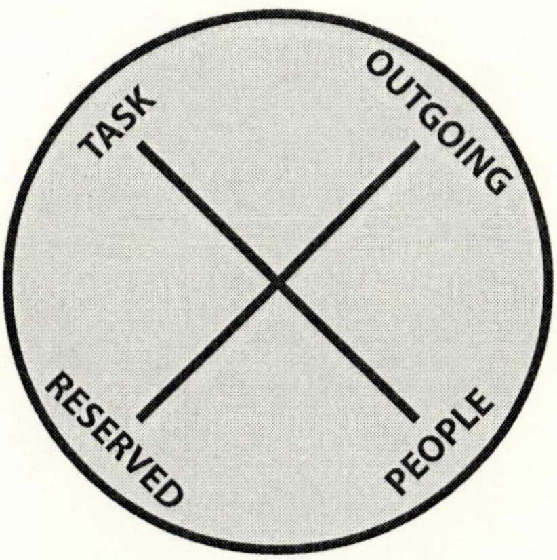

Let's begin to place each specific region in the four quadrants to determine the unique perceptions and behavioral styles. By now, you might have a good idea where you and maybe even your clients tend to lean. As we previously stated, the four specific regions are **DOMINANT**, **INTERACTIVE**, **STEADY**, and **CALCULATING**. (For a quick reference guide on how to sell to each region go to Appendix C in the back of your book.)

When pace and priorities are combined, we begin to see the unique areas within ***the Client Nation.*** You will find that all of ***the Client Nation***'s regions share two traits, just as most of us share traits from both parents. These are combinations of pace and priority. They are outgoing-task, outgoing-people, reserved-task and reserved-people. When these are added to body language and vocal tones, you will have discovered the common language of each region. Let us look at a sky view of ***the Client Nation*** and see how the regions fit within.

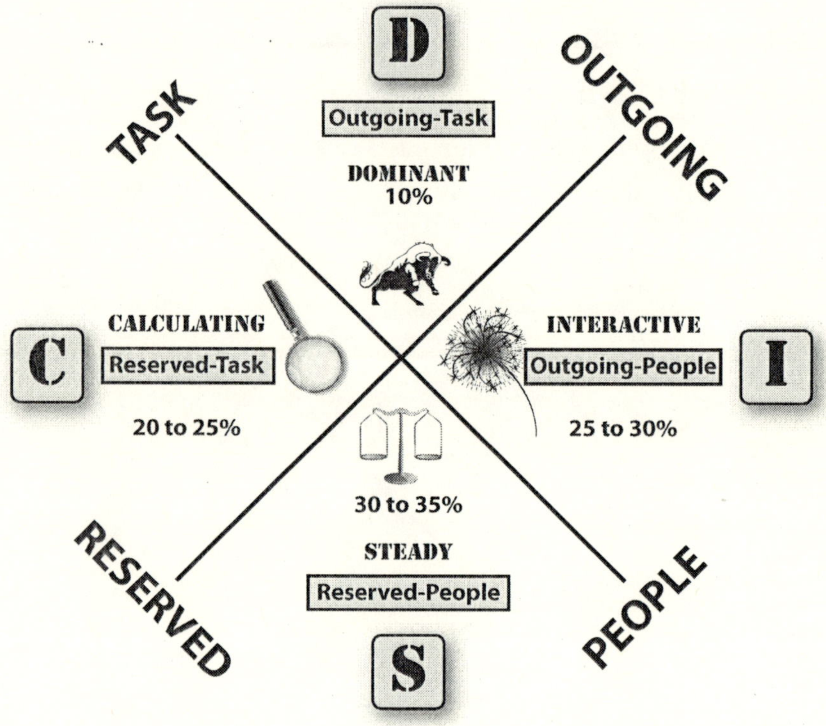

The Client Nation

CHAPTER 5

The DIRECT Region

D

DOMINANT:

Outgoing and Task

Overview	Outgoing-Task
Percentage of Population	10%
Describing Words	Dominant, Direct, Demanding, Decisive, Doer
Symbol	 The Bull – Strength and Power
Reason They Buy	To accomplish a task or project
Pace	Upbeat, fast, intense
Fuel	Results
Need from You	Choice, bottom line answers, control, do what you say you are going to do.
Comfort Zone	Fast, bottom line, getting things done. They buy — they get in and they get out.

Speaking the DOMINANT Client's Language

This is the most powerful region in ***the Client Nation.*** These clients are big picture thinkers and like to create things. The Bull represents strength and a driven focus. A bull who is charging will not veer or quit until it has accomplished it's task, which is why Wall Street uses the term "bull market" to indicate a market that is climbing higher despite the odds or challenges. That is probably why these clients make up only 10% of the population. Any more and we would have constant fights for power. They are the complete pictures of strength. **DOMINANT** citizens *(D's)* are movers and doers. They make the world go around. Their focus is the task and they are dynamic leaders. They never say die.

Some examples are Clint Eastwood (as a cowboy or Dirty Harry), John Wayne, Queen Elizabeth, General Patton, Judge Judy, Bobby Knight, and Tiger Woods.

"A business like an automobile, has to be driven, in order to get results."

BC FORBES

Words that Describe a D

- Driven
- Doer
- Dogmatic
- Demanding
- Direct
- Dominant

DOMINANT types can complete amazing amounts of work and be critical of poorly performed tasks. They also believe that approval and encouragement can lead to complacency. Due to their direct nature they might unintentionally intimidate others. You will find that every region has a fuel or a defining need that makes those clients tick as well as a blind spot that creates their biggest challenge. **D**'s need one thing to accomplish their tasks and to get up in the morning. It defines the air they breathe and their reason for living. **RESULTS!**

"Superhuman effort isn't worth a damn unless it achieves results."

ERNEST SHACKLETON

Going back to my personal trainer story, when my clients were not getting results, I took it personally, I became discouraged and my business suffered. Once I had the right clients and they began to get results, I became energized and refocused. I began to do more and to be the best. As clients, **D***'s* are driven to buy as long as the purchase helps to accomplish a desired result. They go in knowing what they need, buy it, and get out. A friend of mine buys the same kind of car every three years—a Cadillac. He knows what he wants, picks it out, test-drives it, and if he likes it, he buys it. The salesperson asks him, "How many payments do you want to have?" He says "One" and pays cash. That is how a **D** client buys—quickly and decisively.

Blind Spots

Every behavior style and person has unique strengths that make success in sales attainable. These same strengths, when pushed to extremes, can become blind spots. A blind spot is simply an area where you need some assistance to "see." Unfortunately, most of us do not realize where it is until it is too late. As business owners, this awareness is the *key* to better sales and improved repeat customers, so every region's blind spot will be designated not as a negative aspect of the region but as awareness.

"You cannot beware unless you are first aware."

The blind spot tends to be the area we know the least about. Most of our successes stem from understanding our blind spots. The behavioral blind spots we tend to have are typically diagonal from us on ***the Client Nation*** map. We also tend to marry people from the blind spot areas. (Some of you are laughing because it is true.)

My biggest success came when I began to approach all sales and my family from an **S** or the **STEADY** perspective. I began to treat and see people from the **STEADY**-style perception. I was friendlier, listened, and had more compassion and understanding. Don't get me wrong; I was not pretending to be an **S** or manipulate my clients. Nor did I stop being a citizen of the task region. I recognized that 65% of the population is people oriented and my blind spot was that I was coming across too aggressively and task-focused. That approach was affecting sales and repeat business. Remember, what determines success in any business is the client. My behavior would always leave a wake of upset people creating twice the work for me. I learned to speak their language, appreciate their efforts, and treat them with the kind of respect they valued thereby creating the comfort zone they needed to buy from me and refer me. I changed my task from getting the job done no matter what, to getting the job done by serving my clients no matter what they needed. This created more profits in less time and a large loyal client base that told everyone of my services. I still accomplished the task but in less time and with less stress.

If you recall the story of my wife in Costa Rica, you'll remember that one word could mean the loss of an opportunity. It is important for business owners and direct sales professionals to recognize that connecting with your client's pace can make the difference in many sales. A fast-paced salesperson working with a slower-paced client can blow the sale because the two are not connecting. The salesperson may have the right intent by being enthusiastic in helping the client. The client may think the salesperson is pushy and wonder "Why is he so mad?" which could lead to "I really don't like that person." The salesperson may feel frustrated because the client is slow, doesn't seem to know what he wants, or takes too long to decide.

68% of your communication is through nonverbal cues. Some cues - moving fast, pointing, and large gestures—could scare off approximately 60% of your clients who perceive that as aggression. Recognizing your blind spot and how it may affect your client is truly the key to relational sales. This alone will increase the value of your product or service.

Selling to a High D

For **DOMINANT** clients, the value comes from how your product or service brings results and solutions to their task or project. These citizens need:

- Choice
- Challenge
- Control

During the sales process, you must earn the **DOMINANT** client's trust. Some simple ways you can do this are to be punctual, ask questions that pertain to the results she is seeking, focus on how your product or service provides solutions to her needs, and let her control the sales process. This builds trust and allows the client to see the perceived value of your product or service as it pertains to her needs. When selling to this type of client the ultimate trust factor is asking for the sale. They are ready to buy, but because they need control they will challenge. This is your signal that they are interested. Ask them, *"Is their anything else you need to make a decision?"* and provide them what they need and follow up with *"How would you like to pay for that?"* You just earned their respect and most likely their purchase.

Here are some do's and don'ts when selling to a DOMINANT client:

Under stress the D client will react

- Aggressively
- Competitively
- Abrasively

The DOMINANT client does not like

- Indecision
- Slow activities

- Talk without action
- Unproductive activities
- Up-selling
- Not being asked for the sale

The DOMINANT client wants you to be

- Quick
- To the point
- Confident
- Specific
- Respectful
- Results driven
- Able to provide solutions to their needs

Coaching Points

As a DOMINANT business owner, be aware of your blind spots.

Remember:

- People are important. They *are* your CLIENTS!
- Focus on the client's pace to connect and get the results you want.
- Listen to the client's needs and wants.
- It is the client's perception that gets the sale, not what you think he wants or needs.
- 65% of your clients may be people-oriented. Their priorities are feelings and relationships. In other words, they are

> buying the experience you or your sales staff provide. Their perception tends to be *"Are you building a relationship I can trust or just trying to sell me something?"*

When selling to **DOMINANT**-style clients, remember that they know what they want. They don't shop, they buy, and if they ask questions, they only need bottom-line answers. They are straightforward and to the point. The **D***'s* expect to be treated like VIP's and will only refer business to those they trust.

1. Do not be late as this is a sign of disrespect.
2. Let your client dictate the pace and direction of the sale.
3. Focus on how your product or service creates solutions and results to their pain or task.
4. Most importantly, ASK FOR THE SALE. They will buy on the spot if they see the benefit.

Name three clients that tend to be in the DOMINANT region.

1. ______________________________
2. ______________________________
3. ______________________________

What will you do differently the next time you sell to these clients?

____

What DOMINANT Clients Are Saying

Here are the responses that a **DOMINANT** client gave during our interviews about purchasing and referring businesses.

1. **What products are you loyal to and why?**

"There are many products that ensure loyalty from me. Some of the top brands that I go to first are Nikon, Sony, OXO, and Apple. I shop these brands for quality over price, though I don't mind getting a good deal and saving money. But I do believe quality and customer service outweighs a good deal. These products have consistently provided me with exceptional quality and sustainability."

2. **What was the best personal shopping experience you have had? The worst?**

"The best shopping experience I have had was at the Apple store. I have been able to take care of my shopping needs quickly and efficiently. In addition, I have never been hounded to purchase or upgrade anything while I shopped. I consider myself an informed consumer so I do not need anyone to try to up-sell or convince me to buy something else. However, anytime I have asked questions regarding a product, I have received good information from friendly and, more importantly, knowledgeable staff.

The worst shopping experience I have had was at well-known "do-it-yourself" national retailer. In fact, their employees were unhelpful and, at times, rude. Whenever possible I will go to an Ace Hardware. I find them to be extremely knowledgeable and helpful. In addition, if they do not have what I need, they will order it. In one instance they brought it to me at work! As a side note, one of the things that made the national retailer experience so bad is that they treated me as if I didn't know anything about home improvement (which I do because my dad is a contractor). I don't know if this is a gender stereotype or not but it feels like one. I also found the people who work there think they know something but seem to only have enough information to up-sell or refer a certain product and I believe they are not that knowledgeable about the project I am trying to complete."

3. **What helps you decide to buy a product or service?**

"Quality, good customer reviews (when available), a good report from *Consumer Reports*, and my own past experience with the company or product—i.e. good customer service—and not treating me like an uninformed consumer."

4. **When do you decide to refer a product or service?**

"I make a point to give good feedback to a product or company when I have received excellent and exceptional service. I will often suggest products and services to my family and friends if I have had a good experience with them. I have posted links on FaceBook as well as service sites like Angie's list and the websites where I purchase products."

5. **If you could talk to every business owner, what would you want him or her to know about you as a client?**

"Don't assume I am uninformed because I am a woman. Do not assume I want to buy a different product unless I have expressed interest in it. Treat me as you would your best customer despite the way I look or what I am wearing. Pay attention to the small details—they are what make me come back over and over. I have been going to the same jewelry store for 14 years. I will not go anywhere else because they provide exceptional service. They know me, my tastes, and treat me as if I can buy anything in the store, even if I can only afford the $20 earrings."

MICHELLE
Atlanta, Georgia

This should give you a good understanding of the needs, perceptions, and behaviors that make up a **DOMINANT**-style client. This region can be a highly intense, and sometimes scary, place to visit. If you can speak the language and know how to provide the benefits, results, and solutions these clients are seeking, they will buy on the spot.

"Be willing to make decisions.
That's the most important quality in a good leader."

GEORGE S. PATTON

Now let's leave the outgoing and task region of **DOMINANT** and head over to the outgoing and people region of Interactive. This area is where FUN is born and the party never ends. Everybody MAMBO!

"I never did a day's work in my life.
It was all fun."

THOMAS A. EDISON

CHAPTER 6

The INTERACTIVE Region

I

INTERACTIVE:

Outgoing and People

"People rarely succeed
unless they have fun in what they are doing."

DALE CARNEGIE

Overview	Outgoing-People
Percentage of Population	25%–30%
Describing Words	Inspiring, interactive, involved, impressive
Symbol	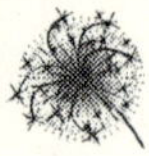 Fireworks - They light up the room and need to be the center of attention.
Reason They Buy	Image and Popularity
Pace	Fast and Energetic
Fuel	Fun
Need from You	Recognition, smiles, to be liked
Comfort Zone	Fun, exciting, prestige, friendly. *I's* want to know WHO? Who else is wearing it or using it? Who will see me?

Identifying the INTERACTIVE Client

The **INTERACTIVE** *(**I**)* client is easy to spot; just follow the loud laughter and talking. She loves to be the center of attention. Whether it is one person or a large crowd, this type thrives on contact with people. They tend to be the WOO HOO people in the crowd. Gaining everyone's acceptance, love, and admiration gives this type energy. This region can sell ice to an Eskimo and make it sound so exciting that the Eskimo will bring his friends to buy as well.

I'*s* tend be loud, happy, and optimistic. They have the knack of getting close in a very short period of time and can make you feel like you have been friends forever. The **I**'s are quick with a bright smile that illuminates the room. They can always share a funny story to help you forget your worries. These clients have a "larger than life" energy and personality and they are not easily forgotten. They will speak fast and often of many topics in one sentence. They are compassionate and are people pleasers. The most important quality you can ever offer an **I** type is **RECOGNITION**. Give them praise and they will love you forever.

Some examples are Howie Mandell, Robin Williams, Jay Leno, Oprah, Bill Cosby, Lucille Ball.

Words that Describe an I

- Inspiring
- Involved
- Impressive
- Interactive

Any combination of these traits can cause **I** clients to set the World of MouthOnomics ablaze with good or bad press. They love to write letters to owners and supervisors to make sure everyone knows what a good or bad experience they had. They may be only 25%–30% of the population, but they control attention and influence the buying decision of all the other Client Nation regions. This can cause an **INTERACTIVE** client's bad or good experience to spread like wildfire and create potential damage or profit to any business. As the old saying goes, "There is no greater wrath than a woman scorned." I think that was said by a business owner on the receiving end of the communication from an upset **I** client.

"What every genuine philosopher (every genuine man, in fact) craves most is praise— although the philosophers generally call it 'recognition'!"

WILLIAM JAMES

Speaking the INTERACTIVE Client's Language

To create an immediate comfort zone, **SMILE**. Deep down most **INTERACTIVE** citizens just want to be liked, and a smile shows them that you like them. Laughing and being personal will set them at ease. Making them feel special will also go a long way with this client. Compliment them; they like to feel that they are the center of attention. Treat them as VIPs and friends. By making them feel like the only client in the store, you will show them that they are important customers. Don't misunderstand these clients. They may love the spotlight and being the center of attention, but this does not necessarily make them snobs or too good for the masses. Yes, there are some like that, however, **I** clients tend to be the most appreciative and genuine towards people who treat them nicely. They are the first to unselfishly share with others without expecting anything in return. Remember, this is their comfort zone and natural tendency. The more fun and special the environment, the higher the perceived value you are creating for these clients.

"If you obey all the rules, you miss all the fun."

KATHARINE HEPBURN

Selling to an I Client

It is important to remember that **INTERACTIVE** clients tend to live in the moment. These clients have the unique gift of multitasking. In their minds, there are always three TV screens going on at the same time and they are all interconnected. These screens consist of the conversation they just had, the conversation they are having, and the conversation they will have because of what they are doing right then. There is nothing wrong with this. This is how they are wired and what makes them tick. This is important to know since the experience you provide will influence their future conversations. **INTERACTIVE** clients love a warm and friendly sales staff. They are also very influenced by others. When they see your product or service, they really want to know who else is using it.

My wife is part of the **INTERACTIVE** region. The following shopping experience personifies the **I** client.

> "When our children Alex and Rebecca were very young, I was at home with them quite a lot. I greatly enjoyed being a mommy but I also craved being around people. So staying home for extended periods of time did not work well for me. My husband can definitely attest to this fact. When Alex went to preschool, I would put Becca in her car seat and off we would go to the mall, very often day after day. We would frequent many stores, but *Baby Guess* had the cutest baby clothing for both boys and girls. All the people knew me since I was there on a regular basis, and I liked that they were always happy to see me. They made me feel special. I loved the way everyone commented on how Alex and Rebecca always wore the nicest clothes. I felt like an awesome mom. Overall, it was just a great experience and a wonderful feeling. One day, I remember it like it was yesterday, I got to the mall and as I was putting 20-month-old Rebecca in her stroller, she looked up at the big Macy's sign and very clearly said one of her first words, "Charge!" I sadly realized that the time had come for these frequent outings to stop."

I now have two **INTERACTIVE** citizens in my household—my wife and my daughter. My home is always fun and my credit card is always missing. But notice what made her want to return day after day. "They were always happy to see me. They made me feel special. I loved the way everyone commented on how Alex and Rebecca always wore the nicest clothes. I felt like an awesome mom." The experience of her treatment and the compliments on the kids' clothes were a direct reflection of her and how she felt and, more importantly, why she was a loyal return customer and told everyone about the store. **INTERACTIVE** clients like honesty and a considerate sales staff. This tells them you care about relationships, rather than being phony and trying to take them for all their money. These clients tend to be non-confrontational and may not tell someone they feel pressured. Do not force them into a corner. If they do not feel like they are having fun, they will feel stressed and will not feel comfortable enough to buy anything. They will also tell everyone of how terrible the experience was in their perception.

The greater the experience, the higher the accolades they will share with their friends through the superhighway of the World of MouthOnomics. These particular clients can be your biggest advocate and promoter if you take the time to treat them as VIPs and genuinely develop a friendship and relationship with them. The time spent will be rewarded a hundredfold by their promotion of your product or service.

Here is a recap of the INTERACTIVE region.

Issues that often cause stress and could stop the buying process for **INTERACTIVE** types are

- Rejection
- Public embarrassment
- Loss of social standing and recognition
- Highly structured environments
- Rude or inattentive salespeople

- Pressure sales and a snobby or technical environment

The INTERACTIVE client needs

- Recognition
- Approval
- Popularity

A stressed I client might

- Talk faster than usual
- Exhibit uncontrollable and nervous laughter
- Be overly emotional
- Change subjects or divert from the original topic
- Constantly tell jokes or stories to lighten the mood

The INTERACTIVE client does not like

- Being Ignored
- Sarcasm
- Being ridiculed
- Rudeness
- Isolation
- Conflict

The I client wants you to be

- Fun
- Upbeat
- Honest

- Personable
- Enthusiastic
- Attentive

Blind Spots

As an **INTERACTIVE** business owner, be aware of your blind spots. Remember:

- Managing your time is essential.
- Listening provides opportunities.
- Completing tasks is just as important as going to lunch with friends.
- Some clients just want the bottom line and the facts, not stories or a relationship, and that is okay. It is not personal. It is their comfort zone and language.

Coaching Points

When selling to **INTERACTIVE** clients, think in terms of "WHO." *Who* is going? *Who* will be there? *Who* will they see? *Who* will see them? Their basic fuel is fun and they are motivated by recognition. They are driven by social interaction, making them the kings and queens of the social media platform. They look for the people who are going to make this fun and then tell everyone if it was and why or why not.

1. Focus on them and how your product or service will make them feel.
2. Smile and make them feel as warm as you would a long-time friend with a VIP touch.
3. Be honest and genuine.

Remember that they shop for the experience you are providing. The perceived value is you and what you are doing to build a relationship. They will connect the experience of buying to the product or service they are purchasing and it will be that experience they will share with others with dramatic flair. Make it a good one!

Name three of your clients who tend to be in the INTERACTIVE region.

1. ______________________________

2. ______________________________

3. ______________________________

What will you do differently the next time you sell to these clients?

____

What INTERACTIVE Clients Are Saying

Here are the responses that an **INTERACTIVE** client gave during our interviews about purchasing and referring businesses.

1. **What products are you loyal to, and why?**

   "Tide HE; it gets my clothes nice and clean and smelling good, just the way I like them.

   I also got a free one year's supply with my new washing machine."

2. **What was your best personal shopping experience? The worst?**

   "Best – High-end department stores; the stores and the service. The sales staff treats me like a VIP.

   Worst - Stores where I can't find what I am looking for

or with rude salespeople."

3. **What helps you decide to buy a product or service?**

   "Cost and the usefulness of the item or service to me."

4. **When do you decide to refer a product or service?**

   "Service. When I understand and like the product. When I trust the person selling it."

5. **If you could talk to every business owner, what would you want him or her to know about you as a client?**

   "You need to be honest to keep a client. You need to show you care and want to understand."

As we leave the land of fun and spotlights, catch your breath and be prepared for a region of tranquility and serene bliss. The **STEADY** region is full of love and compassion and believes in just taking it slow and smelling the roses along the way with a great group of friends. MMMMMMMM.

"As human beings, our greatness
lies not so much in being able to remake the world...
but in being able to remake ourselves."

MAHATMA GANDHI

CHAPTER 7

STEADY:

"The best and safest thing is to keep a balance in your life,
acknowledge the great powers around us and in us.
If you can do that, and live that way, you are really a wise man."

EURIPIDES

Overview	Reserve-People
Percentage of Population	30%–35%
Describing Words	Steady, stable, sweet, status quo
Symbol	 The Scale - Represents balance. They are always in the middle as they do not want to hurt anyone's feelings and want everyone to get along. They bring balance to any relationship or business.
Reason They Buy	Relationship. Familiarity with product. A feeling of comfort and security with sales staff and business.
Pace	Slow
Fuel	Supporting others and peace and balance.
Need from You	A sense of security, familiarity, and appreciation.
Comfort Zone	Patience, consistency, predictability, no conflict, relational and familiar.

As I mentioned in the **DOMINANT** region, my biggest success came from understanding my blind spot and learning to adjust to it. I learned to speak the **STEADY** language when it was necessary to build relationships. My greatest accomplishment came with my daughter. As I mentioned before, we are a blend of all regions. Her predominant behaviors are in the **INTERACTIVE**, **STEADY**, and **DOMINANT** regions (which translates into a very strong-willed drama queen). She was very sensitive about her feelings and protective of others, never hesitating to express how she felt.

For 10 years we fought over everything. It seemed we could never do anything that did not end in a fight. At 14 years old, my daughter was having trouble identifying her feelings, so she would lash out. I was fortunate enough to learn human behavior and soon realized what I was unknowingly doing to create this war zone. I realized my voice, deep and forceful, sounded as if I was yelling at her, even when I was speaking in a normal tone. Talking to her face-to-face made her feel uncomfortable and combative. So I adjusted. I spoke more slowly and lowered my voice. I listened and waited. I sat next to her with my arm around her and asked questions. In 48 hours I repaired ten years of war. She is now 21, in college, and we speak every day. I have taught her to cook and even had a shoulder for her to cry on. By simply speaking her language and seeing her perspective, I now have a great relationship with my daughter.

Speaking the STEADY Client's Language

The **STEADY** *(S)* client likes a calm, easygoing environment where there is a predictable routine and things remain pretty much the same. These people thrive in an environment where bonding with individuals is possible. They are the peacekeepers; they will often do anything to keep the peace with little or no regard to how it may affect them. They are always behind the scenes to ensure everything runs smoothly and, most importantly, that everyone's needs are met. They may feel like they are imposing and monopolizing your time. Reassure them and show them appreciation for being your clients. Go out of your way to earn their trust. This will pay major dividends; they will be the most loyal clients you will ever have. If you do not take advantage of them and/or treat them or others rudely, they will make sure to tell everyone they trust about you. Their friends will listen since they know **STEADY** types do not make decisions lightly.

Some examples are Dr. Martin Luther King Jr., Gandhi, Mother Teresa, Mr. Rogers, the Dalai Lama.

Words that Describe an S

- Supportive
- Stable
- Cautious
- Kind

The **STEADY** client loves predictability and harmony. These people are stable and like doing one thing at a time. Because **S** clients desire security, they love supporting others and want to know that your business will be there for them. This behavioral style is non-confrontational and will avoid arguing like the plague. To give you an idea of their mindset, they view the debate team in school as odd. They might say, "Why would anyone want to argue for competition?" or "I avoid arguing like the swine flu and here are people trying to get on a team to argue and to win at it. That is crazy." The **STEADY** clients are very dependable. They love routine because it makes them feel comfortable—like Mom's apple pie or a baby blanket. They know what to expect. This creates that secure feeling. They do not like surprises.

A friend of mine from the **STEADY** region once told me the way he would relax after a very stressful day was to go home, get comfortable, and watch his favorite movie, one that he has seen over 100 times. When I asked him why the same movie, he said, "I know what happens in every scene and I know how it ends." These clients are loyal to any business that provides continuity and desires to build a long lasting relationship with them.

"Loyalty is still the same,
whether it win or lose the game;
true as a dial to the sun,
although it be not shined upon."

SAMUEL BUTLER

Selling to a STEADY Client

The STEADY client will go to the same coffee shop at the same time and order the same items. The staff will get to know the client and develop a relationship. This client knows that every time he goes in the staff will know his name, what he likes, and what to expect. His affinity for sameness makes him an ideal loyal and advocating client. One of my STEADY type friends loves sushi. He kept talking about how we should go and hang out and have sushi. So I accepted. As soon as we walked into the restaurant, everyone knew his name. The waitress brought him his favorite drink. The Sushi chef had his appetizer ready with his own set of chopsticks. My friend had been going to this place every Wednesday for ten years. He knew what to expect and the staff knew what he liked and how he liked it. Nothing had changed.

The service was outstanding and so was the time spent with my friend. I have visited this restaurant several times and referred it even more. That is the power of an advocating loyal client, especially an S-style client. Imagine if you had 30 to 50 S clients who purchased your product or service on a regular basis without fail and referred you to everyone they thought could benefit from your business. What would that do for your business and cash flow? Can you feel the sense of security and ease that would create?

Here is a recap of the STEADY region

The S client needs

- Appreciation
- Security
- Assurance

Issues that cause stress and stop the buying process are

- Conflict

- Confrontation
- Abrupt changes
- Being rude to someone else in front of an **S** client
- High pressure sales or salespeople

The **STEADY** region contains the largest remorse buyers. Since these clients are non-confrontational, they will buy the product or service to prevent hurting the salesperson's feelings. Before you ever get home, they will have cancelled the service or returned the item. They avoid stress or stressful situations as this shuts them down.

Unless they feel comfortable, they may hesitate to express how they feel. This will cause this client not to buy and even avoid your business altogether.

Under stress the S client will react with

- Procrastination
- Indecision
- Silence
- Withdrawal (shut down)
- Completely avoiding the person, location, or situation
- Nervous laughter
- A quick exit
- A glazed look (deer in headlights)

The STEADY client does not like

- Insensitivity
- Intense conversation
- Sarcasm

- Being pushed
- Surprises
- Misunderstandings

In order to build a relationship that will earn his business, the STEADY client wants you to be

- Kind
- Pleasant
- Caring
- Patient
- Understanding
- Gentle

Blind Spots

As a **STEADY** business owner, be aware of your blind spots. Remember:

- Some changes are good.
- Not all aggressive customers are angry with you. They may be interested in what you have to say.
- It is okay to say NO!
- You don't have to be taken advantage of just to serve your client.
- Some relationships are based on results and not necessarily on friendships or feelings.
- How you help some clients accomplish their tasks is how they build relationships.

Coaching Points

When selling to **STEADY** clients, pace and patience is the key. Their loyalty and referrals can be an extreme asset to any business.

1. Be gentle and focus on relationships. Establish a safe, secure, and consistent location or product for them to purchase.
2. Be patient. They do not make quick decisions.
3. They are focused on supporting others.
4. They value relationships more than the product or service.
5. They are the biggest remorse buyers.
6. These clients will be the most loyal to you if you take the time to build a genuine relationship with them.
7. They are part of the people-oriented population, so the sales experience is important. The experience is tied to you and how you treat them. Not the product or service you are selling.

The **STEADY** region is 30%–35% of the population, the biggest population of ***the Client Nation***. More often than not, you will be speaking to a Steady type. They take time to consider everything and go along with what the majority decides. They will ask everyone they trust for his or her thoughts, so be patient. If you ask them a question, wait. Don't speak. Give them time to think about the answer.

Name three of your clients who appear to be of the STEADY region

1. ____

2. ____

3. ____

What will you do differently the next time you sell to these clients?

____

____

"It's the steady, quiet,
plodding ones who win in the lifelong race."

ROBERT SERVICE

What STEADY Clients Are Saying

Here are the responses that a Steady client gave during our interviews about purchasing and referring businesses.

1. **What products are you loyal to and why?**

   "Crest toothpaste, because it truly cleans my teeth."

2. **What was the best personal shopping experience you have had? The worst?**

   "Best – Skin care and cosmetics. Same product for 18 years."

3. **What helps you decide to buy a product or service?**

   "If the salesperson is nice, if I know the product, and that the store or product purchase is convenient."

4. **When do you decide to refer a product or service?**

   "If I have tried it, I like it, and I like the salespeople.

If it works for me and I had exceptional service."

5. **If you could talk to every business owner, what would you want him or her to know about you as a client?**

   "I want to build friendships/relationships and then I want to see, over time, if there is a fit."

Notice that this client did not mention any specific negatives. She did not want to offend; she would rather avoid the product or service altogether than to offend anyone.

Out of the hundreds of interviews and focus groups we conducted with this type of client, rarely did this group say a negative word. By the same token, if these clients heard someone put down the competition or someone else, they would be done with that product, service, or person. You would not know they were gone; they would just fade into the night like a shadow. If you have a client that seems to have fallen off the face of the earth and will not return your calls, emails, letters or any other form of communication, then he or she may be a **STEADY** client.

For a **STEADY** client, the comfort zone is created by taking the time to know her as a person and being genuine about assisting her with her needs. No matter how often she comes back to try the same product or others like it, she will eventually be your most loyal and constant client. If you see these clients as a long-term investment and not a short-term nuisance, you will have a strong and stable foundation of intensely loyal and **STEADY** customers.

As we leave the serene and caring region of the **STEADY** citizens, we now venture into the final and logical region of ***the Client Nation***. The **CALCULATING** region is the smartest of all the regions. They are technically advanced and focused on task and logic. Mr. Spock from the Star Trek TV series is a good example of the **CALCULATING** region. Live long and prosper.

"Logic is the beginning of wisdom, not the end."

LENARD NIMOY

CHAPTER 8

The CALCULATING Region

C

THE CALCULATING REGION:

"The cautious seldom err."

CONFUCIUS

Overview	Reserved-Task
Percentage of Population	20%–25%
Describing Words	Cautious, competent, careful, conscientious
Symbol	 The magnifying glass. They like to investigate and research everything.
Reason They Buy	Quality products or services to assist them in accomplishing their project.
Pace	Slow and Precise
Fuel	Quality answers, process, and procedure
Need from You	Ability to research independently, excellence and value. Individual focus and attention, knowledgeable staff.
Comfort Zone	Structure, accuracy, details and correctness. Logical and simple online research and buying procedures.

Speaking the CALCULATING Client's Language

The **CALCULATING** *(***C***)* citizen of this region carefully explores all options and studies all related information. These clients will validate the quality of information and develop procedures, which will prevent mistakes. They love graphs and analyzing facts. Their cognitive skills allow them to think of ways to improve an idea. They will go to any length to achieve excellence.

This region is very thorough in everything they do, which is why **C** type clients ask a lot of questions. They will have done countless hours of research and comparison before deciding what to buy. The word perfectionist can best describe them. Think of Sherlock Holmes and his powers of deduction, which were always based on research and facts. "Elementary, my dear Watson, elementary."

Some examples are: Sergeant Friday, Einstein, Sir Isaac Newton, Mr. Spock, Steve Jobs, Sherlock Holmes, Leonardo da vinci, Benjamin Franklin, Bill Gates.

Words that Describe a C

- Cautious
- Competent
- Careful
- Conscientious

The **C**-client is seldom wrong and double-checks everything to make sure it is that way. This is a very expensive lesson a mentor of mine once learned. He had just completed a small workbook and hastily put it together so he could have it for a big convention coming up. He paid $1 a book to print and bind it. He ordered forty thousand and had them shipped to the convention. After a presentation to a large arena, many ran to the table to purchase his workbook for the second part of the live training. He sold ten thousand books the first round.

At a break during the second period, many participants came up to him to point out spelling errors, grammatical errors, page errors, misprints, missing pages and on and on. It became so bad, he had to refund everyone their money and throw out the remaining thirty thousand books. At $1 a book that was thirty thousand dollars thrown in the dumpster. With refunds, his original investment of $40,000 was lost. He then hired an editor with strong **CALCULATING** region traits and has made money ever since without incidence. The **CALCULATING** editor made sure everything was right and was of the highest quality.

"Quality means doing it right when no one is looking."

HENRY FORD

C types tend to be extremely analytical. They plan the work and work the plan. These clients will most likely know more about your product or service than you. If they did not initiate the sales process, they will not buy immediately. They will gather information and research it later, double-checking for accuracy. These clients require trust through fact verification before they can build a relationship and rapport. Their comfort zone comes from accurate information, quality answers, and a process or procedure they can follow. Like the **DOMINANT** region this region does not shop, it buys. The clients get in, get what they need, and get out. These people, in particular, would rather buy online, as they are not fond of human interaction. That does not make them bad people. It is simply how they are wired and what makes them tick. If they do venture into your store, ask them how you can assist them in their buying process, and provide them with exactly what they are looking for.

They tend to ask many questions about every detail. Provide accurate and relevant information. Let them direct the buying process. Your focus should be on the product or service and the client's need for it.

Selling to a CALCULATING Client

The CALCULATING client is

- Focused on excellence.

- Dedicated to the buying process.
- Very logically driven.
- Attentive to details, including your body language and what you say.
- More engaged in a one-on-one experience.

The CALCULATING client likes

- Consistency
- Detail
- Procedure
- Quality

The C type client does not like

- Being criticized
- Mediocrity
- Being questioned
- Sudden changes
- Unnecessary interruptions
- The up-sell or being told what to buy and why

The C client wants you to be

- Accommodating
- Accurate
- Reasonable
- Accountable

- Knowledgeable of the product or service you are selling
- Honest
- Sincere
- Structured
- To the point

Issues that cause stress and stop the buying process are

- Being criticized
- Mistakes
- Disorganization
- Generalities
- Inaccurate answers or guesses
- Up-selling
- Pressure sales
- Disrespectful and/or inattentive salespeople

Under stress, the C client will

- Ask precise questions
- Be very picky
- Be pessimistic
- Refer to research and facts to validate the point
- Display impatience
- Judge
- Be stern

- Ask or point to the rules
- Leave the store or simply walk away

Blind Spots

As a CALCULATING business owner, be aware of your blind spots. Remember:

- Most of the clients you may encounter are people-oriented.
- Not all clients make decisions based on fact; they tend to make decisions on how they feel about you and how you treat them.
- Feeling is a logical conclusion to purchasing for some clients.
- Not all clients are interested in every minute detail or a history lesson of your product or service.
- Business is relational first, supported by technology second.
- 68% of your communication is nonverbal. You can at times appear cold and uncaring. Smile!
- 65% of your client base may be people-oriented. It is logical to provide them what they need in the manner they need it, in order to accomplish the task at hand.
- 80% of today's purchases are based on someone's referral, rating, or testimonial (based on a study by Nielsen's Ratings). The experience you provide will determine what your clients say to influence others to buy or stay away from your product or service.
- Without a client there is no cash flow, and therefore, no business. Make sure you connect with the client.
- Clients won't care how much you know until they know how much you care.

"Wisdom is only effective when you care enough to put it into action."

RICO PEÑA

Coaching Points

When selling to **CALCULATING** clients, it will be difficult to see any emotion. They have the ultimate poker face, void of emotion and expression. If at all possible, they would rather avoid human interaction altogether. This client often uses self-checkouts. If they do decide to venture into your store, they would rather have a clean, effective process to purchase without much fuss. The process should be logical and step-by-step.

These clients are often misunderstood as cold and uncaring. But that is far from the truth; they are simply operating from the logical point of view, and in most cases logic is void of emotion. Just as all the other regions in ***the Client Nation*** have a unique common language, logic, process, and procedure are the common language of the **CALCULATING** clients. They are the agents of organization and rules. These clients are the all-knowing cab drivers of the super highways of the World of Mouthonomics. Technology is their second language. They use blogs, social media, videos, and the Internet as their source of information, expression, and research.

Just like the **INTERACTIVE** client, the **CALCULATING** client can be a powerhouse in what he says about your business. This is an ideal client to have to skyrocket online sales if you can provide all the tools, research, and smooth operating procedures for him to do so.

"Success is a process more than a realization."

ANONYMOUS

Name three of your clients who seem to be part of the CALCULATING region.

1. ______________________________

2. ______________________________

3. ______________________________

What will you do differently the next time you sell to these clients?

____

____

What CALCULATING Clients Are Saying

Here are the responses that a **CALCULATING** client gave during our interviews about purchasing and referring businesses.

1. **What products are you loyal to and why?**

   "A1 Steak Sauce - Tastes great.

   Heinz ketchup - Thick and sweet tasting."

2. **What was the best personal shopping experience you have had? The worst?**

   "Best - Dillard's was my best shopping experience. I was given one-on-one individualized attention.

   Worst – A department store where the clerks could not

answer any of my questions and acted like I did not exist. I left."

3. **What helps you decide to buy a product or service?**

   "Quality, value, service.

   When all my questions are answered satisfactorily and the salesperson is genuinely concerned with my needs for the products."

4. **When do you decide to refer a product or service?**

   "By the value provided.

   When I am respected, treated fairly, and the quality of the product is good."

5. **If you could talk to every business owner, what would you want him or her to know about you as a client?**

   "If I see the value of the product, I am a very loyal customer.

   Treat all clients with respect; treat them as if they were the most important person in the world. As the old adage goes, the customer is always right."

CALCULATING clients know they know what they know. They have done their homework, researched the facts, and will follow them carefully. They are both task and logical thinkers. They think in terms of "bottom line." They are cautious by nature and will not make any decisions rapidly. They can analyze a situation in an instant and see what is really going on behind the scenes. They are natural body language readers and can pick up inconsistencies with what you say and do. Here is a recap of the **CALCULATING** client.

1. They are slower-paced, critical thinkers; they need time to think things through.

2. Do not push or up-sell.

3. You must earn their trust through quality, accurate answers, and excellent customer service.

4. They are happy being alone and only tend to interact with people when necessary.

5. They prefer technology and books to socializing.

6. Focus on the product or service as they tell you they need it and then provide it.

7. They respond well to organization, process, and procedure.

8. They prefer one-on-one interaction

As Joe Friday used to say on the show Dragnet, "Just the facts, ma'am, just the facts." That is a **CALCULATING** citizen of ***the Client Nation***.

You have now seen an overview of all four regions of ***the Client Nation***: results and performance-driven **DOMINANT** region; fun and outgoing **INTERACTIVE** region; loving and supportive **STEADY** region; and finally the analytical and factual **CALCULATING** region. All of these regions possess unique abilities. If you were to organize them into a team for work, sales, or direct marketing, they would be a force to be reckoned with. The **D***'s* can cast the vision and lead the team to it. The **I***'s* are great starters and can sell and promote to everyone they meet. The **S***'s* are great finishers and support the others with anything they need. The **C***'s* make sure to ask the questions that should be asked and make sure everything is done with perfection, quality, and by the book.

Imagine them working in perfect harmony. You would have a team that provides tangible results, concrete loyal customers, and a quality product or service that is beyond anything the competition or the client ever would have expected. Would that be an advantage to a business, team, or sales force? I know it would. How to find and organize such a team is the topic of my new book *The Chemistry of Team Work*, a deeper look into the behavior of a perfect team and how to duplicate it.

Now that you have a better understanding of the client's perception, language, and comfort zone, let's look at how to identify each region when you meet new clients in order to connect with their perception. This will allow you to connect with him and build a stronger relationship quickly and effectively.

"Quality in a service or product is not what you put into it. It is what the client or customer gets out of it."

PETER DRUCKER

CHAPTER 9

Reading Your Client

"The **language** *of the* **body** *is the key that can unlock the soul."*

KONSTANTIN STANISLAVSKY
RUSSIAN ACTOR AND CO-FOUNDER OF THE MOSCOW ART THEATRE

We are constantly bombarded in every direction with an immense amount of information from television, radio, phones, Internet, video games, newspapers, magazines, and so much more. To give you an idea of just how much information we digest on a regular basis, here is what a recent university study had to say. The study concluded that one New York Times Sunday edition newspaper contained more information than an adult male in the 18th century knew in his entire lifetime. One newspaper, one day. one form of communication. Due to the tsunami of information our minds have adapted to, we must decide what has important relevance to our immediate needs and attention. The rest is just white noise.

You have only three seconds to make an impact on any client. The following information will provide you with the tools to quickly identify what region the client is from and how to make a connection. With practice, you will be able to jump into any language required by the client. Just as with any new language, the more you practice, the better you will communicate and thereby create a comfort zone that will result in loyal return clients, quality referrals, and advocates of your product or service. (See Appendix B for charts.)

As we have discussed throughout the book, perception is reality. It is important to note that this also applies to body language and vocal tones. Our perceptions are based on all the data and experiences stored in our lives to this very minute. Our decisions are based on all the data we have experienced, learned and seen up this very moment. For example, a **DOMINANT** person may not have any problems seeing things from a **DOMINANT** perception but may have trouble seeing things from a **STEADY** perception. It is like having two individuals wearing glasses with different color lenses. The one with green lenses might say, "Isn't the green sky beautiful today?" while the other person with purple lenses would say, "It's not green, it's purple!" As far as their perception is concerned, each one is correct. Without exchanging glasses and experiencing the other person's perception, they will argue that they are right and the other person is wrong.

Has that ever happened to you? You were absolutely sure of something, but no matter how much you tried to convince someone else of your point, the other person still argued that you were wrong? You are both right, based on the data you each have, your opinion is correct. Unless a neutral source introduces new data that would contradict or support one or the other, you will both be right. This is important to remember when speaking to clients. In some cases opinions are formulated even before we say a word. Over 68% of what we say is through nonverbal communication. Imagine the perception others have of you before you even say a word. By understanding the body language and vocal tones of your clients, you can then quickly identify the region they tend to belong to and adjust your blind spot to see that client's perception. More often than not, we fail to do so. Below is an example of what can happen when we do not take the time to see the client's perception.

During training with a large corporation on how to improve their customer approval rating and increase their loyal client base, a sales manager told us this story.

Tom was a high **D** salesperson working for a non-profit organization raising money for their charity. He had set up interviews with different potential donors. His deadline was that day at 5 p.m. and he was $250,000 short of his goal. This was the last appointment of the day and the last name on the list. Being a seasoned salesperson, he knew what he had to do to close the deal. He was meeting with Sam, a high

S business owner, to present the proposal for the non-profit organization. During the presentation, Tom used soft tones and focused on the pictures of the family and dog. He made sure not to invade Sam's space and kept his hand movements down to a minimum so they would not seem out of control. He approached slowly and softly. He pointed out all of the people Sam would help and how everyone would be so appreciative of his generosity. Since Tom remained in control of his natural tendencies and focused on his pace and gentle body language, he was connecting with Sam's common language.

At the end of the presentation, Tom looked at the clock on the wall and saw that it was three o'clock, so he went in for the kill and asked Sam, "What do you think?" Sam took a moment to consider and as he did, Tom leaned forward and kept staring at Sam as if trying to will him into signing. After what seemed an eternity to Tom, he began to go over the benefits again but in a faster and more intense tone. Tom's body tensed and his hands began to keep pace with his tone. Sam immediately sat back and seemed nervous at Tom's sudden change in demeanor. Irritated, Tom leaned forward and asked, "This is everything you were looking for so why are you so apprehensive?" Sam responded, "I am just not sure I understand how my contribution will be used to help others." Tom was now even more impatient. The veins in his neck were bulging and his nostrils began to flare. He looked at Sam, similar to the way a bull looks when being taunted by a red cape. "Sam," he said, "trust me, this is exactly what you are looking for. There is not a better place for you to invest your money and I don't understand why you just don't see it!" Sam, visibly agitated, told Tom, "I need some time to consider your proposal." Tom asked Sam in a loud and forceful tone, "How much time do you need? Can we close this today?" But Sam seemed unprepared to close that day or any other day, for that matter. He agreed to meet back with Tom in two days, and he promptly cancelled the next day. Tom's body language and change of tone made a big impact on Sam's decision to invest. Tom forgot that it was about the client, not about himself or the deadline.

Body Language

We all communicate using body language. Studies show that 68% of what we say is through body language. That's pretty chatty. The body provides you with visual cues as to what the client likes or doesn't like and if she is comfortable or needs more information. This lets you adjust as necessary.

The visual clues provided by your clients give you a hint as to where they are on the map of ***the Client Nation.*** We have created a chart that allows you to quickly identify the region, priorities, and even the needs of your clients just by learning how to read their body language. This will give you the edge to immediately assess what you need to engage the clients in order to create their specific comfort zones allowing them to feel comfortable enough to buy.

Learning the body language of each region will also allow you to determine the specific language to use to connect quickly with the client before you even say a word. This provides you with the confidence that you are about to create a connection that will result in a sale or a referral. Remember, this will take practice. By using this book as a reference guide, you will see that you will be able to identify and know what to say and do in order to naturally connect with any client at any time.

Body Language

DIRECT

- Steady Eye Contact
- Big Gestures
- Quick Movements
- Leans Forward
- Points

INTERACTIVE

- Animated Expressions
- Much Body Movement
- Often Distracted
- Energetic
- Charming, Personable

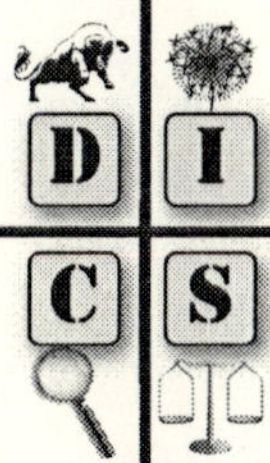

CALCULATING

- Few Facial Expressions
- Controlled Gestures
- Faultless Grooming
- Non-Emotional
- Formal, Conservative

STEADY

- Intermittent Eye Contact
- Wears Subdued Colors
- Gentle Gestures
- Exhibits Patience
- Polite, Non-Confrontational

Information provided by ***Sell Naked Systems***® **www.sellnaked.com**

Vocal Tones

Understanding the client's pace is by far the quickest way to identify his region. You can do this simply by listening to their vocal tones. Some are fast, others slower. Some are stronger, others softer. By learning to listen to and identify the tones, you will be able to connect them to the outgoing or reserved aspects of ***the Client Nation.*** When you combine pace with body language, you can determine the predominant region this client is comfortable in and the priorities, buying signals, and comfort zones. This is also the easiest way to connect with any client. If he speaks quickly and loudly, you speak quickly and loudly; if he speaks softly and timidly, you speak softly and timidly. Take the time to pay careful attention to your client. He will tell you everything you need to know about his pain and what he really needs. Your job as business owner and sales professional is to listen and provide a solution, benefit, or result in a way that your client sees value.

Vocal Tones

DIRECT

- Talks more than listens
- Blunt and to the point
- High volume, fast speech
- Makes strong statements
- Uses forceful tones

INTERACTIVE

- Dramatic
- Tells stories, anecdotes
- Much inflection
- Shares personal feelings
- High volume, fast speech

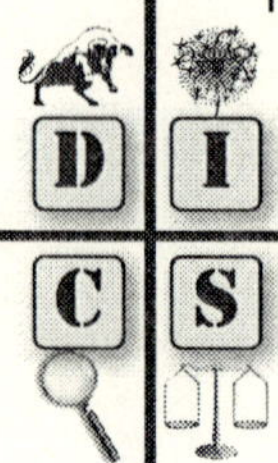

CALCULATING

- Fact oriented
- Asks pertinent questions
- Monotone
- Uses "thinking" words
- Likes speech to be precise

STEADY

- Prefers Listening
- Lower volume, slower rate
- Last one to speak
- Stops quickly if interrupted
- Warm, conversational tones

Information provided by *Sell Naked Systems*® **www.sellnaked.com**

Congratulations!

You have just completed level one of "Speaking Client." You are now prepared to venture into the sales arena, confident you have the tools and resources necessary to begin to connect and communicate with many different clients in their native language, while getting the results and profits from your business, with less effort in less time. I advise that you practice. Just as with any language, if you do not keep practicing, you will forget. You do not want to be like that person who took Spanish in high school and believes he can speak it because he adds *O's* to the end of every word—"The door-O", "The hotel-O." Not very pretty, is it? Or like my wife in Costa Rica, who almost missed finding the bathroom in time by one word.

You now have all the tools necessary to speak fluent Client. You have seen the client's perception and his comfort zones. You have seen how our own blind spots can create some of the challenges that may cause the client not to buy or even generate bad press. You have seen the power of the World of MouthOnomics and how it can benefit or hinder your bottom line. Through this journey, you have experienced the emotional and logical reasons clients buy, as well as what regions they are part of when purchasing or referring.

In the preface, I stated that you would receive three benefits, results, or solutions by applying or reading this book.

1. Make your product or service enticing to every client.

2. Create a referral machine that will drive more business.

3. Apply simple skills to identify the buying motivators of every client.

I hope you have seen and applied the benefits, results, and solutions the answers in this book have provided you. I also asked you three questions:

1. Would your business benefit if you could know what your client was thinking?

2. How often have you walked away from a sale or presentation wondering if the client was really interested in buying?

3. What would you pay to have your clients fall in love with your product or service and tell everyone about it?

I hope that after reading my book the answers to these questions are positive and far more profitable than when you began reading. I also promised to show you how to connect, communicate, and create relationships. The trip through each region showed you the clients' priorities, behavioral styles and, most importantly, what fuel can create a sale and ongoing referrals. And finally, you saw the roots of the client's native language, the hidden clues in body language and voice tones.

We have shown you from the client's perception the advantages of providing results, benefits, and/or solutions. You also learned the benefit of knowing how to create a comfort zone. This allows you to develop the kind of relationship with your clients that create advocates and return clients. You now have all the tools and insights to know what the client really is thinking and what he needs. But all this information is irrelevant if it does not create more sales and a stronger client base, right? (See appendix A, B, & C for quick reference guides.)

In my opinion, the final piece of the puzzle is closing the sale. This last layer will make sure you are always ahead of the competition and will increase your loyal client base through exceptional service and relational sales. This, for me, clearly defined the true nature of every client, the core needs, and what I had to do to provide solutions, benefits, or results that caused the client to be incredibly loyal and a loud and positive spokesperson for my business. I learned how to cement success with every customer. Simply understanding how to walk in your client's shoes will benefit your business beyond your own expectations. HOW? That is level two of the "Speaking Client" course. (Visit **www.clientnation.ning.com** for a sneak peak.)

I have always been accused of giving away too much free information to my clients. So I figured, why stop now? As a token of my appreciation for buying this book, I am offering you a bonus chapter—***"The clients' M.R.I.** (the Mind, Reason, and Intent of why they buy)"*—accessible only on my web site. This chapter gives you further insight and applications behind the psychology of why the client buys. This will give you a great edge over the competition. You will be able to read more about this in our CLIENT NATION blog, *"The Art of Exceptional Expectations"* at **www.clientnation.ning.com**

Here is how you receive your bonus chapter:

1. Go to **www.theclientnation.com**

2. Click on **Bonus Chapter**

3. Enter code: **I AM A CITIZEN 2010**

You will be able to download the e-book of the bonus chapter available only to my readers.

There will be a section where you can tell me what you think about the book and the bonus chapter. After all, this is ***the Client Nation*** and you are a citizen. I want to hear your voice. Give me your opinion, no matter how honest it is, about the book and what you would like to see next at **www.clientnation.ning.com**.

I have dedicated my life to helping those who wish to succeed, find clarity, and make their passion a reality. I wanted to give you a perspective from the client's point of view that would be useful and enlightening. There are so many lost opportunities, lost dreams, and unnecessary stress due to lack of knowledge and simple understanding on how to communicate effectively with each other. You now have that knowledge. Apply it with a servant's mind and heart and serve your clients with the confidence that you are building a lasting relationship. Provide the kind of service that reflects your passion and exceeds their expectations. **If you don't take anything else from this book, remember this:**

*"Wisdom is both
the ability to discern what is best
and the strength of character
to act upon that knowledge."*

KING SOLOMON

Appendix: A

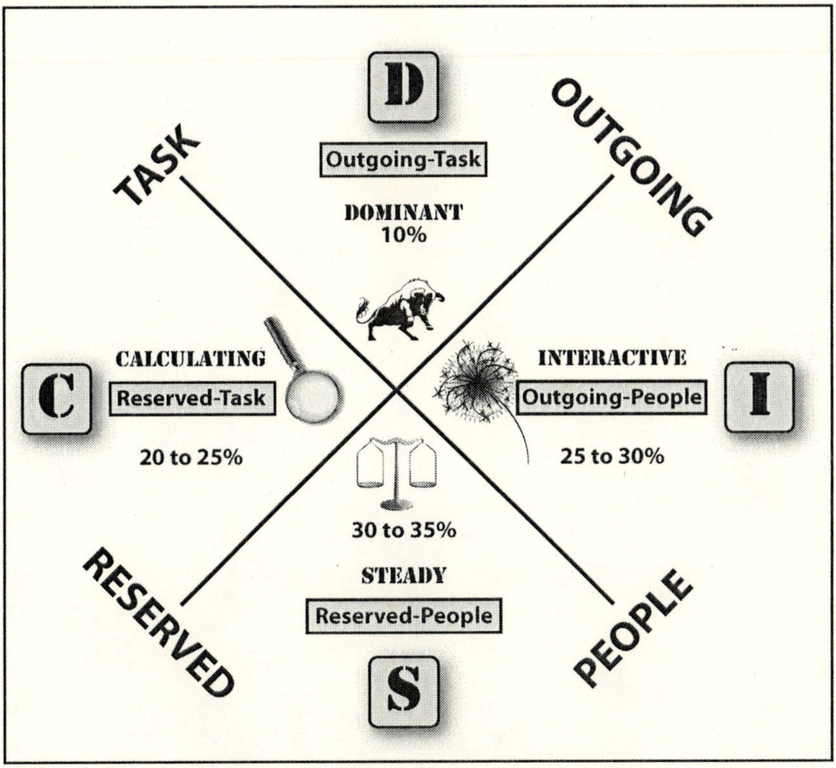

The Client Nation

"Striving for success without hard work
is like trying to harvest where you haven't planted"

DAVID BLY

APENDIX B

DOMINANT

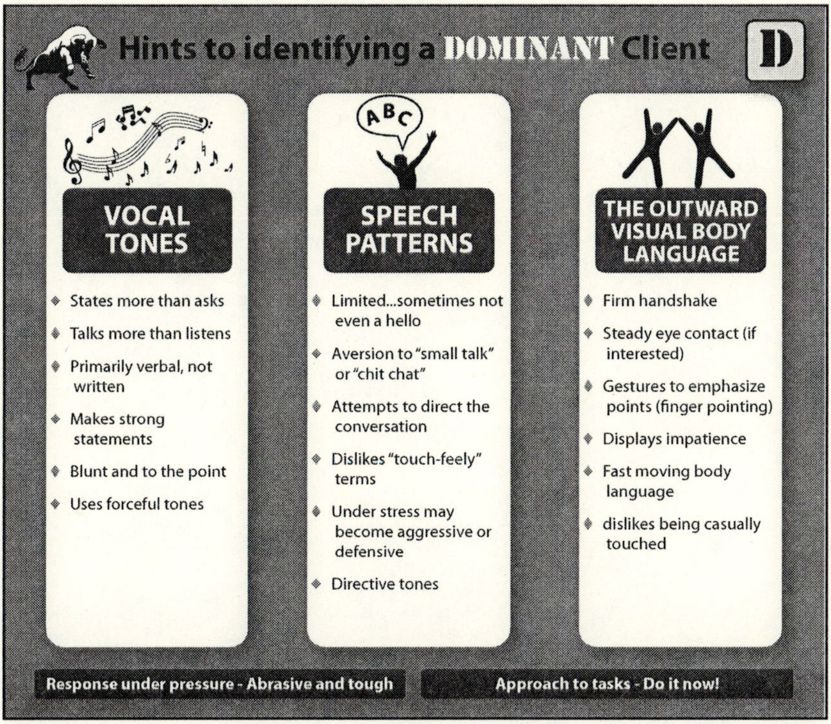

INTERACTIVE

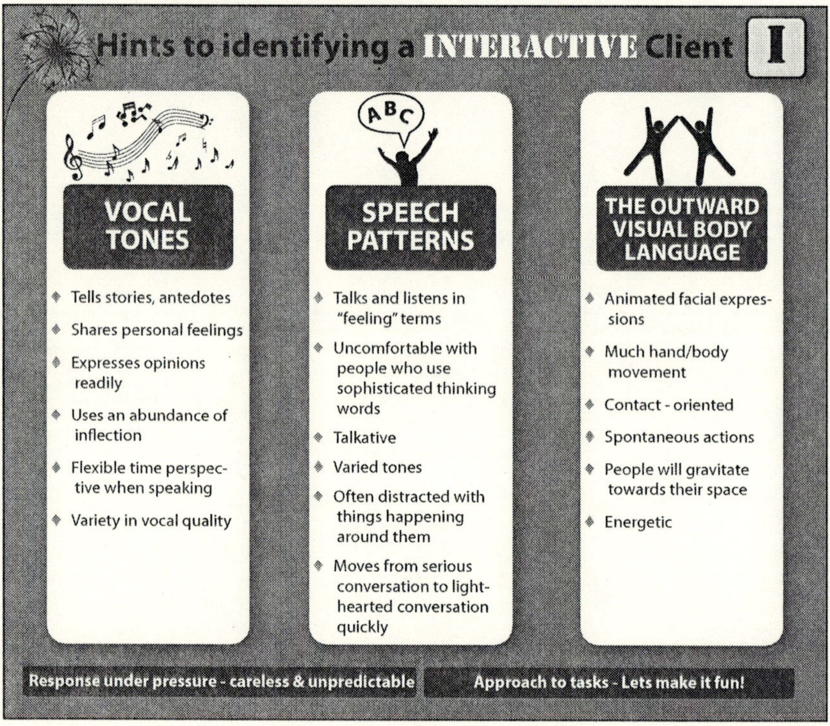

STEADY

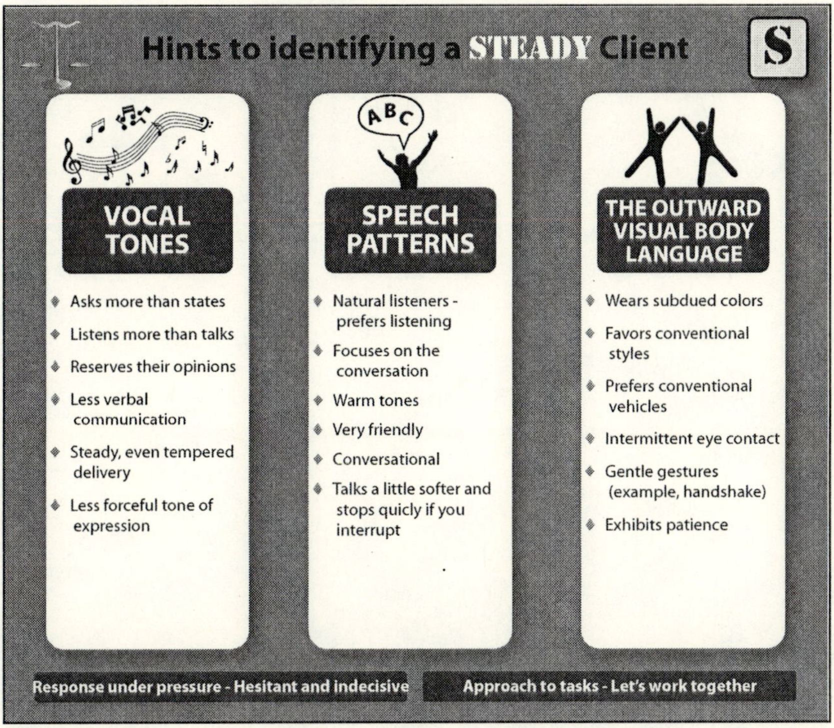
Hints to identifying a STEADY Client
S
A B C
VOCAL TONES
Asks more than states
Listens more than talks
Reserves their opinions
Less verbal communication
Steady, even tempered delivery
Less forceful tone of expression
SPEECH PATTERNS
Natural listeners - prefers listening
Focuses on the conversation
Warm tones
Very friendly
Conversational
Talks a little softer and stops quicly if you interrupt
THE OUTWARD VISUAL BODY LANGUAGE
Wears subdued colors
Favors conventional styles
Prefers conventional vehicles
Intermittent eye contact
Gentle gestures (example, handshake)
Exhibits patience
Response under pressure - Hesitant and indecisive
Approach to tasks - Let's work together

CALCULATING

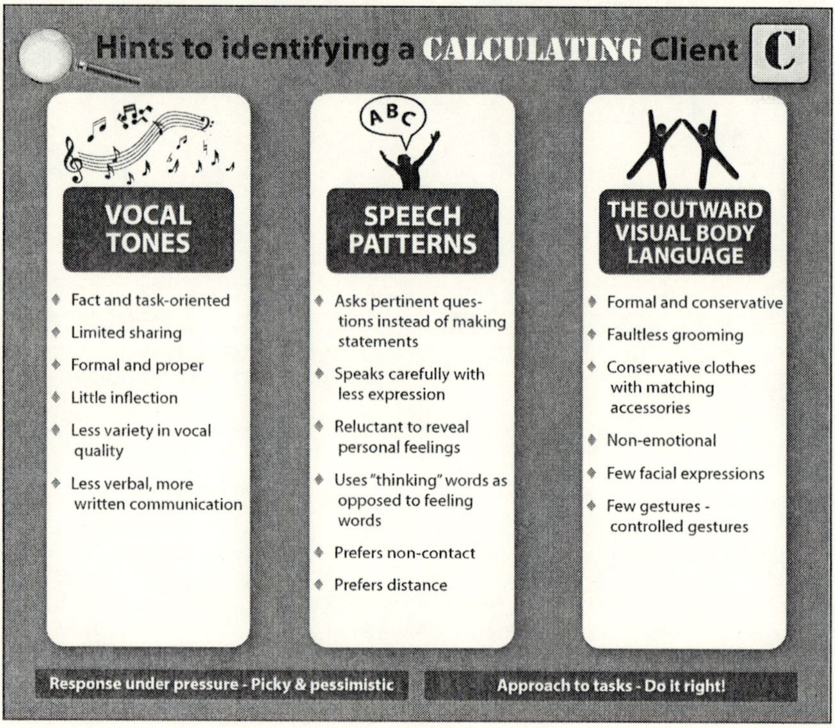

Appendix C

Tips for Successful Selling to Each Region

(From the "Connection phase' at the **Sell Naked System**® *3-day sales boot camp)*

D

To Connect

- Pace: Fast
- Priority: Task
- Need: Results
- Build: Trust
- Words that connect: Performance, Producing, Results
- Build trust by returning phone calls promptly, arriving on time and getting to the point
- **DOMINANT** clients are attracted by strength

When Selling to a D

- Look the client in the eye
- Be direct; don't beat around the bush
- Stand or sit erect
- Maintain a business-like attitude
- Give the client choice, challenge, and control in order to buy

I

To Connect:

- Pace: Fast
- Priority: People
- Need: Fun
- Build: Relationship
- Words that connect: Image, Fun, Popular, New
- Use testimonials, picture, stories, and samples
- **INTERACTIVE** clients are attracted to those who lavish them with attention

When selling to an I

- Have fun
- This is as much a social visit as a sales presentation
- Be noticeably enthusiastic
- Smile, even while you are talking
- Give the client recognition and approval in order to buy

S

To Connect:

- Pace: Slow
- Priority: People
- Need: Security and similarity
- Build: Relationship
- Words that connect: Team, Ease, Similar and Together
- Build relationships; they want you to be sincere
- **STEADY** clients want to be part of a team

When Selling to an S

- Slow down
- Wait 4-5 seconds for the response
- Use products that are familiar or recognizable as examples
- Be kind; do not put down another business or person
- Give the client appreciation, security, and patience in order to buy

C

To Connect:

- Pace: Slow
- Priority: Task
- Need: Quality answers and procedure
- Build: Trust
- Words that connect: Plan, Process, and Procedure
- Build trust by being credible; quote research studies
- Calculating clients are interested in procedures and following sound logic

When Selling to a C

- Be precise and well-prepared
- Have documentation that will support your claims
- Use logical progression of ideas and incorporate hard data
- Stand or sit erect
- Maintain a business-like attitude
- Give the client quality answers, a slower pace, and a process in order to buy

Glossary

Behavioral style. How a client behaves in the moment.

Benefit. The advantage or value a client receives.

Blind spot. An area that a client is unfamiliar with or unaware of.

Client *(language)*. The pace and priorities used by a client during the sales process.

Comfort zone. A familiar, safe, or comfortable area.

Common language. The pace and priority each behavioral style uses to communicate and establish value.

Feature. A property or characteristic of a product or service.

Fuel. What drives each client's primary behavioral style.

In business for the client. Serving the client's needs beyond the client's expectations.

Pace. The speed (fast or slow) in which each client communicates.

Pain. What burdens the client the most in business or personal life.

People *(oriented)*. A client who is drawn to or focused on people and relationships.

Perceived value. The value based on the client's perceptions, needs, or wants. The benefit, result, or solution the product or service provides to the client.

Perception. The impression based on the client's sense of reality up to that point in time.

Priority. What has the greatest importance or value.

<u>**Region.**</u> A specific location, behavioral style, or client type within ***the Client Nation.***

<u>**Relational business.**</u> Sales and referrals based on the relationship between two clients.

<u>**Relational sales.**</u> Connecting and building rapport with the client's, in order to build a comfort zone for sales.

<u>**Servant mindset.**</u> The desire to serve others and add value with a total disregard for rewards or a "what's in it for me" attitude.

<u>**Solution.**</u> The answer to a need or desire.

<u>**Survival mindset.**</u> Self-preservation and focus on oneself.

<u>**Task**</u> ***(oriented).*** A client who is driven by the need to accomplish an assignment, project, or job.

<u>**The Client Nation**</u> ***(country).*** The collective of the clients' buying needs and desires as a whole.

<u>**World of MouthOnomics.**</u> The combination of word of mouth, economics, and social media. The effect of a client has on a business's profits and losses based solely on what the client shares about their experience with that business.

ABOUT THE AUTHOR

Rico Peña has combined his 25 years of entrepreneurial spirit and the simple understanding of providing the client's needs into a methodology applied today by some of our biggest companies, chambers, and fastest growing direct marketing businesses.

Rico is a specialist in the field of human behavior and an expert in client behavioral strategies. He is a highly sought-after bilingual trainer, speaker, and consultant for companies seeking to increase sales, employee performance, and market penetration. His three-day sales boot camps and workshops, in collaboration with Pici & Pici Inc., have provided many individuals and companies from around the world the clarity and direction they need to increase profits, morale, and client loyalty.

He has been given the *Outstanding Georgia Citizen* and *Honorary Lieutenant Colonel* award by Georgia's former Secretary of State, Max

Cleland, for his work with the music industry and underprivileged children.

Rico is currently the CEO and founder of Peña Global, a behavioral sales and professional speaking firm, and Sensational You, an association dedicated to helping business women launch and grow their businesses in any market place. He is also a master English/Spanish sales trainer for the Pici & Pici Inc. *"Sell Naked Successfully"* Sales System®.

Rico has also appeared in the 2009 *People to Know* Magazine. He served his country proudly from 1989 to 1995 in the United States Marine Corps. Rico is a dedicated father of two children and a loving husband. He currently resides in Atlanta, Georgia.

For more information on how Rico can assist you or your company's sales staff and management team on site or through his 3-day boot camps, visit **www.sensationayou.net.**

Recommended Resources:

Sell Naked on the Phone* | *Sell Naked in Person
Joe and Dawn Pici
www.PiciandPici.com and www.SellNakedSystem.com

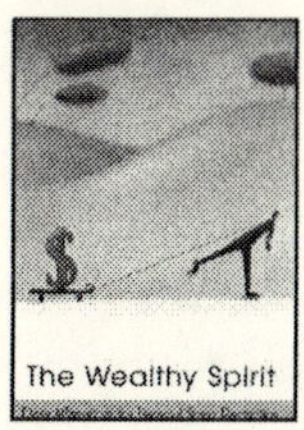

The Wealthy Spirit
Chellie Campbell
Reduce the financial stress in your life.
www.chellie.com

Strategic Acceleration
Tony Jeary
A revolutionary new approach to achieving ultimate success in any business endeavor, from one of the world's top business coaches and trainers.

The Client Nation

Their PERCEPTION, *Your* PROFITS

What the clients are saying you should do
so they will become loyal repeat clients who refer you